$18.95

THE ENGLISH AMERICANS

The Peoples of North America

THE
ENGLISH
AMERICANS

James M. Cornelius

CHELSEA HOUSE PUBLISHERS
New York Philadelphia

On the cover: The opening of the Winnipeg Hunt Club in Manitoba, Canada, in 1913, an example of English culture in the New World.

CHELSEA HOUSE PUBLISHERS
Editor-in-Chief: Remmel Nunn
Managing Editor: Karyn Gullen Browne
Copy Chief: Juliann Barbato
Picture Editor: Adrian G. Allen
Art Director: Maria Epes
Deputy Copy Chief: Mark Rifkin
Assistant Art Director: Loraine Machlin
Manufacturing Manager: Gerald Levine
Systems Manager: Rachel Vigier
Production Manager: Joseph Romano
Production Coordinator: Marie Claire Cebrián

The Peoples of North America
Senior Editor: Sean Dolan

Staff for THE ENGLISH AMERICANS
Associate Editor: Elise Donner
Copy Editor: Philip Koslow
Picture Research: PAR/NYC
Senior Designer: Noreen M. Lamb
Cover Illustration: Paul Biniasz
Banner Design: Hrana Janto

3 5 7 9 8 6 4 2

Library of Congress Cataloging-in-Publication Data
Cornelius, James M.
  The English Americans/James Cornelius.
    p. cm.—(Peoples of North America)
  Includes bibliographical references.
  Summary: Discusses the history, culture, and religion of the English Americans,
factors encouraging their emigration, and their acceptance as an ethnic group in
North America.
  ISBN 0-87754-874-9
      0-7910-0289-6 (pbk.)
  1. British Americans—Juvenile literature. [1. British Americans.] I. Title. II. Series.
E184.B7C65 1990   89-70801 973'.0421—dc20
CIP   AC

CONTENTS

THE PEOPLES OF NORTH AMERICA

CHELSEA HOUSE PUBLISHERS

A NATION
OF NATIONS

Daniel Patrick Moynihan

The Constitution of the United States begins: "We the People of the United States . . . " Yet, as we know, the United States is not made up of a single group of people. It is made up of many peoples. Immigrants from Europe, Asia, Africa, and Central and South America settled in North America seeking a new life filled with opportunities unavailable in their homeland. Coming from many nations, they forged one nation and made it their own. More than 100 years ago, Walt Whitman expressed this perception of America as a melting pot: "Here is not merely a nation, but a teeming Nation of nations."

Although the ingenuity and acts of courage of these immigrants, our ancestors, shaped the North American way of life, we sometimes take their contributions for granted. This fine series, *The Peoples of North America*, examines the experiences and contributions of the immigrants and how these contributions determined the future of the United States and Canada.

Immigrants did not abandon their ethnic traditions when they reached the shores of North America. Each ethnic group had its own customs and traditions, and each brought different experiences, accomplishments, skills, values, styles of dress, and tastes in food that lingered long after its arrival. Yet this profusion of differences created a singularity, or bond, among the immigrants.

The United States and Canada are unusual in this respect. Whereas religious and ethnic differences have sparked intolerance throughout the rest of the world—from the 17th-century religious wars to the 19th-century nationalist movements in Europe to the near extermination of the Jewish people under Nazi Germany— North Americans have struggled to learn how to respect each other's differences and live in harmony.

Millions of immigrants from scores of homelands brought diversity to our continent. In a mass migration, some 12 million immigrants passed through the waiting rooms of New York's Ellis Island; thousands more came to the West Coast. At first, these immigrants were welcomed because labor was needed to meet the demands of the Industrial Age. Soon, however, the new immigrants faced the prejudice of earlier immigrants who saw them as a burden on the economy. Legislation was passed to limit immigration. The Chinese Exclusion Act of 1882 was among the first laws closing the doors to the promise of America. The Japanese were also effectively excluded by this law. In 1924, Congress set immigration quotas on a country-by-country basis.

Such prejudices might have triggered war, as they did in Europe, but North Americans chose negotiation and compromise instead. This determination to resolve differences peacefully has been the hallmark of the peoples of North America.

The remarkable ability of Americans to live together as one people was seriously threatened by the issue of slavery. It was a symptom of growing intolerance in the world. Thousands of settlers from the British Isles had arrived in the colonies as indentured servants, agreeing to work for a specified number of years on farms or as apprentices in return for passage to America and room and board. When the first Africans arrived in the then-British colonies during the 17th century, some colonists thought that they too should be treated as indentured servants. Eventually, the question of whether the Africans should be viewed as indentured, like the English, or as slaves who could be owned for life, was considered in a Maryland court. The court's calamitous decree held that blacks were slaves bound to lifelong servitude, and so were their children. America went through a time of moral examination and civil war before it finally freed African slaves and their descendants. The principle that all people are created equal had faced its greatest challenge and survived.

Yet the court ruling that set blacks apart from other races fanned flames of discrimination that burned long after slavery was abolished—and that still flicker today. The concept of racism had existed for centuries in countries throughout the world. For instance, when the Manchus conquered China in the 13th century, they decreed that Chinese and Manchus could not intermarry. To impress their superiority on the conquered Chinese, the Manchus ordered all Chinese men to wear their hair in a long braid called a queue.

By the 19th century, some intellectuals took up the banner of racism, citing Charles Darwin. Darwin's scientific studies hypothesized that highly evolved animals were dominant over other animals. Some advocates of this theory applied it to humans, asserting that certain races were more highly evolved than others and thus were superior.

This philosophy served as the basis for a new form of discrimination, not only against nonwhite people but also against various ethnic groups. Asians faced harsh discrimination and were depicted by popular 19th-century newspaper cartoonists as depraved, degenerate, and deficient in intelligence. When the Irish flooded American cities to escape the famine in Ireland, the cartoonists caricatured the typical "Paddy" (a common term for Irish immigrants) as an apelike creature with jutting jaw and sloping forehead.

By the 20th century, racism and ethnic prejudice had given rise to virulent theories of a Northern European master race. When Adolf Hitler came to power in Germany in 1933, he popularized the notion of Aryan supremacy. *Aryan*, a term referring to the Indo-European races, was applied to so-called superior physical characteristics such as blond hair, blue eyes, and delicate facial features. Anyone with darker and heavier features was considered inferior.

Buttressed by these theories, the German Nazi state from 1933 to 1945 set out to destroy European Jews, along with Poles, Russians, and other groups considered inferior. It nearly succeeded. Millions of these people were exterminated.

The tragedies brought on by ethnic and racial intolerance throughout the world demonstrate the importance of North America's efforts to create a society free of prejudice and inequality.

A relatively recent example of the New World's desire to resolve ethnic friction nonviolently is the solution the Canadians found to a conflict between two ethnic groups. A long-standing dispute as to whether Canadian culture was properly English or French resurfaced in the mid-1960s, dividing the peoples of the French-speaking Quebec Province from those of the English-speaking provinces. Relations grew tense, then bitter, then violent. The Royal Commission on Bilingualism and Biculturalism was established to study the growing crisis and to propose measures to ease the tensions. As a result of the commission's recommendations, all official documents and statements from the national government's capital at Ottawa are now issued in both French and English, and bilingual education is encouraged.

The year 1980 marked a coming of age for the United States's ethnic heritage. For the first time, the U.S. Census asked people about their ethnic background. Americans chose from more than 100 groups, including French Basque, Spanish Basque, French Canadian, Afro-American, Peruvian, Armenian, Chinese, and Japanese. The ethnic group with the largest response was English (49.6 million). More than 100 million Americans claimed ancestors from the British Isles, which includes England, Ireland, Wales, and Scotland. There were almost as many Germans (49.2 million) as English. The Irish-American population (40.2 million) was third, but the next largest ethnic group, the Afro-Americans, was a distant fourth (21 million). There was a sizable group of French ancestry (13 million), as well as of Italian (12 million). Poles, Dutch, Swedes, Norwegians, and Russians followed. These groups, and other smaller ones, represent the wondrous profusion of ethnic influences in North America.

Canada, too, has learned more about the diversity of its population. Studies conducted during the French/English conflict showed that Canadians were descended from Ukrainians, Germans, Italians, Chinese, Japanese, native Indians, and Eskimos, among others. Canada found it had no ethnic majority, although nearly half of its immigrant population had come from the British Isles. Canada, like the United States, is a land of immigrants for whom mutual tolerance is a matter of reason as well as principle.

The people of North America are the descendants of one of the greatest migrations in history. And that migration is not over. Koreans, Vietnamese, Nicaraguans, Cubans, and many others are heading for the shores of North America in large numbers. This mix of cultures shapes every aspect of our lives. To understand ourselves, we must know something about our diverse ethnic ancestry. Nothing so defines the North American nations as the motto on the Great Seal of the United States: *E Pluribus Unum*—Out of Many, One.

This family of English immigrants landed at Ellis Island in 1906, at the height of the second great wave of European immigration.

THOSE WHO CAME OUT

It is clear that today the United States and Canada are immigrant nations. People from every country in the world have journeyed across the oceans or over national borders to reach America, where they believed they would find things unavailable to them at home—a better job, land or a house of their own, freedom to worship as they wished or to speak their mind without fear of government reprisal, safety from the war and violence that rent their homelands, an opportunity for their children to receive an education and build themselves a better life. For decades, the United States, in particular, has been viewed as the promised land for the literally millions of Europeans, Africans, Asians, and other immigrants who have landed on its shores or crossed its borders in order to make a new beginning. The words of its most revered political texts reveal much about what has made the image of America shine like a beacon to so many around the world—it was, according to the Declaration of Independence, a land where the truth "that all men are created equal" was "self-evident"; it was, according to the Pledge of Allegiance, a land that promised "liberty and justice for all"; it was, according to Abraham Lincoln's Gettysburg Address, a land "conceived in liberty." The notion of America as a haven is central to its self-image: The Statue of Liberty, one of the United States's most enduring national symbols, is above all else an emblem of America's willingness to open its doors to the downtrodden and oppressed of other nations. For many of the millions of European immigrants who entered America at the immigration station at Ellis Island in New York harbor, the Statue of Liberty seemed to welcome them to a land of infinite possibilities, a continent, in the words of the great American novelist F. Scott Fitzgerald, "commensurate to [man's] capacity for wonder."

Indeed, the symbolism represented by the Statue of Liberty informs the notions that many people hold regarding immigration—images and ideas concerning "the huddled masses, yearning to breathe free" who arrived at Ellis Island, mostly from southern and eastern Europe, in the four decades preceding World War I, when an estimated 20 million European immigrants came to the United States. This mass migration, one of the greatest in the history of the world, is often referred to by historians as the second great wave of immigration. It was this generation of immigrants—Italians, Greeks, Serbs, Poles, Ukrainians, Jews, and many others—who provided the manpower for America's Industrial Revolution, who crowded into the ghettos and tenements in America's teeming cities, and whose way of life was documented by such social reformers as the journalist Jacob Riis and the photographer Lewis Hine.

Others, when searching their consciousness for what they know about immigration, might come up with thoughts about the members of the first great wave of European immigration, which took place between 1840 and 1880—the Germans, who now constitute the largest ethnic group in the United States; the Scandinavians, who settled and worked so much of the Midwest; the Irish Catholics, driven by famine and oppression across the sea to the United States, where they introduced religious diversity to what had been a predominantly Protestant nation.

Yet in considering immigration and immigrant groups, many individuals neglect what would seem to be one of the more obvious peoples to spring to mind—the English. This tendency is so prevalent that the English are sometimes referred to as the forgotten or overlooked immigrants, but in the 1980 U.S. census, some 50 million Americans—26.4 percent of the population—reported that they were of total or partial English descent. In more than half of the 50 states, English Americans are the most numerous ethnic group. In Canada, people of completely English descent constitute 25 percent of the population, and 75 percent of all Canadians have at least one English ancestor.

There are many reasons why such a significant group could be overlooked, but perhaps the most important has to do with how early its members arrived on American shores. Most people are simply not accustomed to thinking of the Europeans who first settled North America as immigrants, but in a very real sense they were, for they were motivated to cross the Atlantic and to carve out settlements from the virgin forests of the New World by the traditional incentives that spur immigration—the desire for economic opportunity

The English city of Bristol was a popular point of departure for English emigrants in the 17th and 18th centuries. At the time, Bristol's trade with the American colonies had made it the second largest city in England.

and political and religious freedom. Most prominent among these settlers, particularly in the regions that would become the 13 colonies and then the United States, were the English. Of the 200,000 Europeans who inhabited North America in 1690, 90 percent had themselves "come out" from England or had parents who had done so. Figures such as these provide a clue to another reason why the English are not commonly thought of as an immigrant group: To a great extent, the culture and civilization of the 13 colonies was English. The early civil and political institutions of the colonies were based on English models, most of the colonists belonged to the same Protestant religious denominations as they had at home in England, and they spoke and wrote the English language. They regarded the society that they created as an English one, and they considered themselves to be Englishmen. Indeed, the crux of the dispute that led to the American Revolution was the colonists' anger at being denied one of their fundamental rights as Englishmen, won by the English people over centuries of struggle with the Crown—the right to be taxed only with consent of their elected representative in Parliament. Gradually, of course, colonial institutions took on the characteristics that made them distinctly American, and the process whereby the colonists came to consider themselves American rather than English is the essence of the multifaceted phenomenon known as the American Revolution.

One would think that because it is all but impossible to overestimate the English influence in America, the English would be the least likely immigrant group to be overlooked, but it is the very pervasiveness of the English presence, its familiarity, that makes it so easy to do so. To a great degree, immigrants attracted the notice and sometimes the prejudice and hatred of Americans because they were different—they were shorter, or of a different color, or spoke a different language, or worshiped God differently than more well established Americans. Nativists (those who opposed immigration) charged that the newcomers would not be able to adapt themselves to the American way of life, but in many respects the way of life they championed was an English creation. For these reasons, the English who came to America were regarded less as outsiders than were other immigrant groups. It was during the second great wave of European immigration that the greatest number of English immigrants came to America—some 2 million—but they are rarely thought of as composing part of that migration, in part because they were outnumbered by newcomers from southern and eastern Europe but mostly because in the eyes of the nativists the English did not threaten to dilute America's "native" stock or way of life. According to historian Charlotte Erickson, "English immigrants regarded themselves as belonging to the same ethnic stock as a majority of the native-born whites [in America], and they met few obstacles to participation in the same social and institutional life." So rapid was their assimilation, on the whole, that Erickson believes the English in America were often not sure whether they actually constituted a separate ethnic group. Because all these factors made it that much easier for the English to assimilate and achieve economic success, they were able to become that much more "invisible." But it is this very invisibility that makes the study of the English in America so important, for if the story of any group may be said to be inextricably intertwined with the saga of America, it is the story of the English.

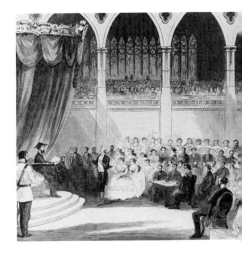

An artist's sketch of the opening of the first Canadian Parliament, in 1867. As is true of the United States, Canada's system of government is based on principles derived from English common and constitutional law.

The crumbling ruins of Hadrian's Wall, which Hadrian, the emperor of Rome, had constructed in the 2nd century A.D. *near the present-day border of England and Scotland to protect the Roman settlements in the south from attack by the Celtic tribes of the north.*

FROM ISLAND TO EMPIRE

If Britain has achieved a prominent role in history, it has done so in spite of its modest allotments. England is a comparatively small island, measuring only about 88,000 square miles. (That figure includes the political divisions of Scotland and Wales, which with England and Northern Ireland constitute the political entity known as Great Britain. For the most part, this book will consider only immigrants from England proper and not the Scotch and the Welsh.) Long before human habitation, England was most likely a part of the European mainland, but it was its character as an island, separated from Europe by the 26-mile-wide English Channel, that was most significant in its development. The Stone Age settlers of England, dark- or red-haired and smallish, probably came from the Iberian peninsula. In the six centuries before the birth of Christ they gave way to taller, light-haired Celtic invaders from northwestern Europe.

Invasions Great and Small

Once he had completed his storied conquest of Gaul (roughly equivalent to present-day France), the Roman general Julius Caesar turned his attention to Britain. Resistance from the Britons greeted his two landings there, in 55 and 54 B.C., and it was not until almost a century later that the Romans were able to establish a permanent presence. It was under Roman rule that the city of London was established as a commercial depot, benefiting from the system of paved roads that the Romans constructed for the transportation of goods and military convoys. Although Christianity made limited inroads during this time, the remarkable thing about Roman rule, according to one archaeologist, was that the Britons "inherited practically nothing" from 400 years of Roman contact. This was in large part because the Romans did not seek to intermarry with or displace the native population but simply to impose their rule from above. The Roman population and influence was never enough to secure the entire English countryside, however, and the result was constant pressure from the non-Latinized Celtic peoples, particularly those residing in the north (present-day Scotland) and the west (present-day Wales). A typical Roman town in Britain was surrounded by thick stone walls to protect its populace from the raids of the Picts and other Celtic peoples.

With Rome itself beleaguered by Germanic tribesmen, by the 5th century it had all but abandoned England, which itself was under repeated attack from a variety of Nordic marauders—Angles, Saxons, Jutes, Danes, and the Vikings or Norsemen. Over time, these invaders turned their attention to settlement as well as plunder, proving themselves as adept as farmers and merchants as they had been as seafaring warriors. From the Celtic resistance to the Anglo-Saxon newcomers was born, among many other legends, that of King Arthur and the Round Table, but despite the opposition of the

This depiction of the evangelist Saint Luke from a set of illuminated gospels at the Lichfield monastery in Staffordshire, England, is typical of the art used to illustrate religious writings in the medieval era.

Britons, the Anglo-Saxons gradually established themselves over much of the island. The period also witnessed the wholesale conversion to Christianity of England of both the Celtic peoples and the Saxons and other conquerors.

Christianity made possible a flourishing of art (in the form of illuminated gospels), learning (in Latin), and music. The development of the church hierarchy and the establishment of bishoprics and parishes facilitated the growth of rudimentary governmental institutions, particularly structures for the collection of taxes and tithes (taxes paid to the church). The most important of the Saxon kings of this period was Alfred of the West Saxons (Wessex), known as the Great for his success in halting the advance of the Danish pirates who had begun to menace England and for his learned and benevolent rule.

The Vikings

The successors to the Danish invaders were the Vikings, who crossed the North Sea in the 10th and 11th centuries in boats holding as many as 100 men, in search of the gold said to be hoarded in England's monasteries.

Marauding Vikings attack the English town of Thetford in this illustration from a 12th-century manuscript entitled English Miracles of Saint Edmund.

Within a generation or two, impressed by the availability of fertile farmland in England, they had established settlements all over the island. From their ranks came the first English king to govern the entire island: Canute, who ruled from 1016 to 1035. After conquering the English, Canute restored them to a place of equality with the Danes, and he was celebrated by monastic chroniclers for his solicitude toward the church, which had suffered cruel depredations at the hands of the pagan conquerors.

By this point, many of the fundamental facets of English life had been established. From the Anglo-Saxons had come a language; from the Norsemen, a system of administration (*law* derives from a Scandinavian word) and skill on the seas and a knack for trading and exploration; from missionaries from Rome and Ireland, a national church. What was lacking was a strong government that would help unite all these disparate elements into a coherent nation.

Feudalism and Magna Carta

That government would be imposed on England from without. Acting upon his claim to the English throne, in 1066, William, duke of Normandy, known to history as the Conqueror, defeated his cousin Harold II at the Battle of Hastings. The prevailing political and social system in Normandy, an area in northwestern France that had been settled, like England, by the Vikings, was feudalism, whereby all land was deemed to be owned by the king or a leading noble, who then granted it, in exchange for pledges of loyalty and military assistance, to the nobles under him. The nobles in turn then granted either land or the right to live on it to the serfs, who pledged their labor in exchange for a guarantee of protection from their lord. Feudalism, which provided the nobility with the labor it needed to work its land, the peasantry with the protection it needed against the rapacity of the times, and the king with the loyalty of his

HIC EXEVNT:CABAI   DENAVIBVS

A section of the Bayeux tapestry, an embroidery that depicts the Norman conquest of England. Queen Matilda, William the Conqueror's wife, is usually given credit for its creation. In this segment, horses are being unloaded from William's invasion barges.

subjects, was imposed by William at the point of a sword during the first years of his reign in England. Those rewarded with the most lucrative fiefdoms from the lands taken in conquest from the English nobility were William's Norman followers. Indicative of the extent to which William was able to impose his control is the Domesday Book of 1086, a precise account of the feudal obligations accruing to him from all over England.

But it is important to remember that for all the evidence of William's absolutism, feudalism was a system of mutual obligations on the part of each class. For example, it was the duty and privilege of the king, in governing, to consult his chief vassals, who were likewise obliged and honored to provide him with advice. In these imprecisely defined responsibilities may be seen the genesis of the conflict that was to dominate English history for the next 700 years—the struggle between the king and his subjects to determine how political power was to be exercised.

Because initially it alone possessed the power to confront the monarchy, the English nobility was in the forefront of the battle for increased political rights. In

1215 it won a crucial victory when it forced the lawless and grasping King John to sign the Magna Carta (the words are Latin for "Great Charter"). The king had aroused the ire of the nobility by his abuse of the traditional feudal methods by which the Crown was entitled to raise money; his popularity was not helped by a series of military defeats that cost the Crown its feudal holdings in France. John had also so alienated the church that he had been excommunicated in 1209 and had been restored to the sacraments only by ceding his entire kingdom to the papacy, which then returned it to him as a fief. Written in Latin, the Magna Carta stated that the king must periodically call a council of his vassals in order to receive their advice and consent on affairs of government. It also provided checks on the king's arbitrary taxation and guaranteed all English citizens freedom from unwarranted arrest and imprisonment, clauses that were later interpreted as the basis for the right to due process, trial by jury, and habeas corpus (that body of the common law intended to prevent an individual from being held illegally; it includes the right to a speedy trial). Another clause provided a council of barons with the authority to enforce, if necessary by arms, the king's compliance with the charter. The Magna Carta is regarded as the cornerstone of England's constitutional liberties because by signing it, King John acknowledged that even the Crown was bound by the rule of law. (The English constitution is not a single written document, like the U.S. version, but is composed of those principles of the common law and statutes that together are held to constitute the rights and privileges of the citizenry and government.)

The Middle Ages

Although the checks on the king's power enumerated in the Magna Carta benefited all the English, the document was concerned primarily with the restoration of traditional aristocratic privileges. For the people, life in the medieval era was, as English philosopher Thomas

Hobbes described life in another context, nasty, brutish, and short. Intense religious faith, as represented by the construction of soaring cathedrals, some of which took the labor of generations to construct, went hand in hand with superstition and ignorance. Bandits roamed England's highways, preying on the unwary. In the latter half of the 14th century, about one-third of England's people died from the dreaded Black Death (bubonic plague). Abroad, England was engaged in almost constant war with France. But the tumult also created new opportunities, as serfs fled baronial manors to work farmsteads left empty by plague and war, and England's constitutional, economic, and cultural institutions continued to develop. Out of the baronial councils gradually developed England's legislative assembly, Parliament, with its two houses, Commons and Lords. Although it was quickly suppressed, the Peasants' Revolt of 1381, led by the craftsman Wat Tyler, demonstrated the willingness of the lower classes to act to secure their political rights. Written in the late 14th century, Geoffrey Chaucer's *Canterbury Tales*, a poetic recounting of a fictional pilgrimage to a saint's tomb at Canterbury, is the period's supreme literary achievement. It remains a peerless evocation of medieval England.

Learning Advances

England's great universities, Oxford and Cambridge, were founded in the medieval era to train priests, but they soon excelled in many disciplines and were attended by the brightest English students and foreign scholars. Like the rest of Europe, England was greatly influenced by the rebirth of learning and artistic activity known as the Renaissance. Historians have suggested that England's tradition as a seafaring nation made its people especially interested in scientific and practical matters, as reflected in the work of countless unnamed mariners, glassblowers, dyers, metallurgists, and other adventurers and artisans during the 16th century. These individuals built on the scientific and technical legacy established by men such as Roger Bacon, who in the late 13th century did pioneering work in logic, mathematics, and human sight, introducing the notion that careful

According to legend, Oxford University was founded in 1167 by disgruntled students from the University of Paris. One of England's two great centers of higher learning, it was initially conceived as an institution for the training of priests.

experimentation and observation must precede theory. England's scientific genius culminated in Sir Isaac Newton (1642–1727), a Cambridge professor and the island's greatest scientist, who built an early telescope, invented calculus, and explained the phenomena of gravity, light, and color.

The House of Tudor

The weakening of the English monarchy, a process that had begun with the Magna Carta and continued through the unrest aroused by England's defeats at the hands of France during the Hundred Years' War (1337–1453) ultimately plunged the nation into chaos. During the Wars of the Roses, which raged from 1455 to 1485, two noble factions—the House of Lancaster, whose badge was a red rose, and the House of York, whose badge was a white rose—battled for control of the Crown. Order was restored with the accession to the throne of Henry Tudor (Henry VII). Ironically, the most significant result of these dynastic struggles was a strengthening of the monarchy at the expense of the nobility, owing in large part to the great loss of life and property that the nobility incurred and the extremely powerful characters of two of the Tudor monarchs.

Henry VIII succeeded his father Henry VII on the throne in 1509 and became the dominant figure of the Renaissance period in England. Henry is often remembered for his outsize appetite, his girth, his divorces, and his six wives, but he was also an intellectual and an astute politician during whose reign the English navy was born, Parliament's power was expanded, and education and learning were promoted. Henry's marital troubles cost two of his wives and several of his ministers and advisers their heads, but his rule was overall a peaceful one, particularly in comparison with the tumultuous times that preceded it. His most enduring legacy is the establishment of the Church of England; when the pope refused to grant Henry the

divorce he sought from his first wife, Catherine of Aragon, Henry obtained Parliament's agreement to the Act of Supremacy, which declared that henceforth the ruling monarch would be the supreme head of the church in England and possess the same spiritual and ecclesiastical authority previously exercised by the pope. The split with the papacy put England in the forefront of the Protestant Reformation, as the movement to reform the church led by Martin Luther, John Calvin, and others was known, but it was representative as well of England's determination to develop and act independently of the rest of Europe.

If Protestantism was the spiritual declaration of England's break from Catholic Europe, then the seas served as the earthly route to independence. During the reign of Henry's daughter Elizabeth I, which lasted from

King Henry VIII established the Church of England when Pope Clement VII refused to dissolve his marriage to his first wife, Catherine of Aragon. Ironically, Henry had earlier been awarded the title Defender of the Faith by the same pontiff for his writings against the Reformation movement begun by Martin Luther. This particular painting, with Henry enthroned at center and his daughter Elizabeth I at his left, is an allegory of the Tudor succession.

1558 to 1603, England challenged the other naval powers—Spain, France, and the Netherlands—for control of the sea and the new lands that had been "discovered" by Europeans in the preceding 150 years. Good Queen Bess, as Elizabeth was known, sponsored the expeditions to the New World of Martin Frobisher and Sir Walter Raleigh, who established the first (albeit impermanent) English colony in North America. She presided as well over the expansion of the English navy, which with its defeat of the vaunted Spanish Armada in 1588 stood as the world's strongest, "the floating bulwark of [the] island," as a later parliamentarian called it. Supremacy at sea, which England could rightly claim for the next 300 years, would be the foundation of the British Empire.

Civil War

The fate that Henry VIII had gone to such drastic lengths to forestall—dying without having left an heir to the throne—befell Elizabeth. As a result, she was succeeded on the throne by her relative James VI, the king of Scotland, who became James I of Britain. Timid and arrogant, James promulgated the theory of the divine right of kings, which held that monarchs ruled by the grace of God and were answerable only to heavenly authority. This absolutist thinking did nothing to endear him to Parliament, which also grew disenchanted with the financial corruption that James resorted to in order to support his lavish court. Undeterred, James simply refused to call Parliament into session for years at a time.

Similar excesses continued under his son and successor, Charles I. The most important constitutional issue of the day concerned the Crown's right to raise revenue without Parliament's consent; Charles resolved it by dismissing Parliament for 11 years, from 1629 to 1640. His revenue-raising measures aroused the animosity of much of the populace, and his persecution of the

Puritans, who wished to purify the Church of England of what they regarded as pernicious and lasting Catholic influences, earned him the hatred of members of that group. When in 1641 a reconstituted Parliament demanded the sole authority over forces raised to combat rebellion in Ireland, Charles refused. Rioting ensued, and the king was forced to flee London. The Parliamentarians and the Royalists each raised armies; in the civil war that followed the Parliamentary forces, led by Oliver Cromwell, were victorious. Charles was beheaded in 1649; Cromwell was installed as lord protector of the realm in 1653 and ruled as a sort of military dictator until his death in 1658. The monarchy was restored in 1660, in the person of the deposed king's son Charles II, but never again would it have the upper

On April 19, 1653, Oliver Cromwell (foreground, just left of center) dismissed the remaining members of the Long Parliament (so-called because it had sat without calling elections for 13 years), telling them, according to this Dutch print of the day, "Be gone, you rogues, you have sat long enough."

hand in its struggle with Parliament, as was made evident by the events known as the Glorious Revolution of 1688–89. When the ardent Roman Catholicism of King James II aroused the animosity of virtually all segments of society, the leaders of Parliament entreated a Dutch prince, William of Orange, to accept the throne. James's army deserted him upon William's arrival, and although he was later able, with the help of Irish and Scottish rebels, to mount a campaign, the Williamite forces prevailed. Parliament's political supremacy was then enshrined in statute by the new king's acceptance of the Bill of Rights, which included guarantees of many of the same rights that were provided by the American Bill of Rights about 100 years later as well as a provision that a Roman Catholic would never occupy the throne of England.

No discussion of the Tudor and Stuart period (the Stuart monarchs were James I, Charles I, Charles II, and James II) would be complete without mention of the literary achievements of the day. The Elizabethan age was distinguished by the production of William Shakespeare's early works; during the reign of James I, Shakespeare's towering tragedies—*Macbeth*, *Hamlet*, and *King Lear*—were written and performed and his sonnets were published for the first time. The reign of James I was also notable for the poetry of John Donne, the dean of St. Paul's Cathedral, and for the English translation from the original Hebrew and Greek texts known as the King James Bible, done by a team of scholars commissioned by the king. The most important literary figure of the civil war and Restoration period was the poet John Milton, whose *Paradise Lost* is generally considered the greatest epic in the English language.

Empire and Enlightenment

In 1707 the parliaments of Scotland and England were united, completing the movement toward union that had begun in 1603 when James VI of Scotland assumed the English throne. (The nation was known thereafter as Great Britain.) Ireland remained firmly under English control, as it had for several centuries, and English colonies had been established in North America and the West Indies. For most of the 18th century, sugar, timber, furs, rum, cotton, and tobacco from the New World made English merchants and traders rich. English ships plied the seas, policing the empire.

The dominant intellectual trend of the time, in Europe and in North America, has come to be known as the Enlightenment. The most important aspect of Enlightenment thinking was its emphasis on reason as the basis for human intellectual endeavor; with it came a belief that if reason and scientific principles were applied to human affairs, including the political sphere,

A late-7th-century portrait of the English philosopher John Locke, whose theory of natural rights greatly influenced Thomas Jefferson and many of America's other Founding Fathers. Locke believed that all human beings were born equal, with the freedom to pursue "life, health, liberty, and possessions."

An English political cartoon from 1798 portrays revolutionary France as a murderous figure eager to plant the tree of republican liberty on English soil, which is defended by the British lion, a traditional national symbol.

progress, often measured as the greatest good for the greatest number, would be the inevitable result. England suffered from no lack of outstanding individuals during this period. The economic theories of Adam Smith, who described the "invisible hand" of capitalism in *The Wealth of Nations*, greatly influenced Enlightenment political thought. The efforts of Henry Fielding helped the modern novel take shape; Edward Jenner developed the smallpox vaccine. And two Americans—Thomas Jefferson, with his insistence that governmental authority derived from the consent of the governed, and Benjamin Franklin, with his belief in human perfectibility, his commitment to democratic freedoms, and his devotion to science and empiricism—were equally influential. The fathers of both men had "come out" from Britain to the colonies, and Jefferson's political thought, expressed most elegantly and succintly in the Declaration of Independence, owed a great deal to the work of John Locke, the celebrated English philosopher.

England's defeat of France in the Seven Years' War (1756–63) added Canada and India to its far-flung empire. Trade with the colonies made England the richest and most powerful nation on earth, a status it retained despite the loss of 13 of its North American colonies in 1783. Commerce with America continued, and Britain was saved the cost of administering and defending the American possessions. Between 1794 and 1815, English prosperity was threatened by the French armies of Napoléon Bonaparte, but Horatio Nelson's victory over the French fleet at the Battle of Trafalgar in 1805 enabled Britain to maintain its naval supremacy. Napoléon's final defeat, by English and Prussian troops under the duke of Wellington at the Battle of Waterloo in 1815, ended the French challenge.

The Industrial Revolution

From about 1750 to 1850, English society underwent a remarkable transformation. Technological innovations, chief among them the invention of the steam engine by James Watt and the development of the power loom,

The invention that sparked the Industrial Revolution: James Watt's steam engine.

made possible the mass production of goods in factories. As a result, capital began to replace land ownership as the chief source of wealth; increasing economic specialization led to the decline of the traditional craftsman; the majority of English came to earn their living from industry rather than from agriculture; and the nation grew progressively more urbanized as rural laborers moved to the cities in search of factory work. Collectively, this transformation is known as the Industrial Revolution.

The technological advances initially had their greatest effect in the field of textile manufacturing, but it was not long before transportation was also transformed. Capitalists soon discovered that England's long-neglected roadway system was inadequate for distributing the vast volume of goods that their factories could produce. The new technology made rapid improvements possible. Paved roads were laid, canals were dug to float goods from factory to town, and coastal harbors were dredged for larger ships, but by far the most important innovation was the development of the railroad and the steamship. By 1850 virtually all of England could be reached by the "iron horse," and steamships had shortened the journey to North America, for example, from a few months' to a few weeks' time. Fuel as well as new building materials for all this growth was needed. New techniques and equipment made the mining of coal more efficient, and the production of iron and steel was dramatically upgraded.

The result was unprecedented prosperity for a great number of English citizens, coupled with widespread social upheaval and misery. The migration of the rural populace to cities such as London, which remained the nation's commercial, political, and cultural hub, and to newer industrial centers, such as Birmingham, Manchester, and Liverpool, resulted in housing shortages and an increase in crime and other vice. In their desire to secure a cheap work force, industrialists often

remained unconcerned about social issues, and their employees were usually underpaid and horribly overworked. A significant number of these exploited laborers were children. Many Englishmen and -women were greatly dismayed by the rise of the "dark, Satanic mills" (a description derived from the poetry of Milton) that belched smoke and soot into the atmosphere, the great disparity that arose between the capitalist and the working classes, and by the crowding, filth, and lawlessness in the cities. Some of the most damning literary portrayals of the social inequities of industrial English society can be found in such masterworks of the celebrated novelist Charles Dickens as *Hard Times*, *Bleak House*, *Little Dorrit*, and *Oliver Twist*.

Queen Victoria ruled England from 1837 to 1901, longer than any other monarch. During her reign, Britain reached its height as an imperial power, symbolized by her being named empress of India in 1877.

The latter period of the Industrial Revolution coincided with the first years of the reign of Queen Victoria. During Victoria's reign, which lasted from 1837 to 1901 and was the longest in English history, Parliament acted to curb the worst abuses of the industrial age. Political districts were redrawn to reflect the shift in population, voting rights were extended to the new working class, child labor was restricted, and educational measures were implemented. The prosperity created by the Industrial Revolution resulted in the emergence of a vast middle class. Among the other lasting social changes of the period was an increasing and seemingly permanent secularization of English society. By 1851 less than half of the English regularly attended a church service; by 1900 the number had fallen to one-third. The trend continued throughout the 20th century; by 1990 only about 15 percent of the English attended a weekly religious service, although 75 percent of the respondents in a national opinion poll said that they believed in a god who played a role in their lives.

Perhaps church attendance declined because the English found so much to occupy them in the things of this world. In the late Victorian period Benjamin Disraeli and William Gladstone, the leaders of the Conservative and Liberal parties, respectively, alternated as prime minister. Disraeli served two terms, in 1868 and from 1874 to 1880; Gladstone served two, from 1868 to 1874 and from 1880 to 1885, and then two more after Disraeli's death, in 1886 and from 1892 to 1894. The two men were rivals and possessed of opposing political philosophies, yet under their brilliant leadership England reached its political and economic zenith. By the end of the 19th century, patriotic English were able to boast that their nation commanded an empire over which, as Nobel Prize winner Rudyard Kipling, the poet laureate of British imperialism, put it, "the sun never sets." The British flag flew over 25 percent of the globe; 500 million people came under its dominion.

World Wars and National Decline

In the early 20th century, Britain's power and wealth made it the envy of other nations that aspired to empires of their own. Germany, in particular, wished to establish itself as the foremost power on the European continent and to challenge England for empire. At the same time, peoples within the empires of the European powers, such as the Serbians, who were then under the thumb of Austria-Hungary, aspired to form their own

Londoners emerge from a public air raid shelter during the Battle of Britain in World War II. Prime minister Winston Churchill said of the heroic efforts of England's air force to protect the island from the Nazis: "Never in the field of human conflict was so much owed by so many to so few."

independent nations. After a Serbian nationalist assassinated the heir to the Austrian throne in June 1914, the complex web of alliances that European diplomats had constructed in order to maintain a balance of power on the Continent plunged the world into war. When Austria-Hungary declared war on Serbia, Germany, which was bound to Austria-Hungary by treaty and sensed an opportunity to expand its influence, followed suit. Russia was pledged to defend Serbia, and France and Britain to aid Russia, so they immediately entered

the fray. The result was a conflagration that devastated Europe. Ten million people lost their lives; twice that number were wounded. The spiritual and psychological toll of the slaughter and destruction is impossible to estimate. The British forces alone had 3 million killed or wounded, and a generation of potential leaders was lost. Although England emerged from four years of war as one of the victors, in the postwar years it became evident that much of the nation's human and material wealth had been spent.

England's recovery was slow and was hindered by the worldwide depression of the 1930s. In that decade, unemployment in one English industrial city, Jarrow, reached 75 percent. English preparedness for future aggression was affected by complacency as well as hard times. Having defeated Germany in the "war to end all wars," the English believed that they had quashed any threat to their supremacy, at least from a European nation. Thus, while the increasingly urgent warnings of Parliament member Winston Churchill about aggressive German intentions fell on deaf ears, a resurgent Germany rearmed under the fanatical Nazi dictator Adolf Hitler, annexed lands to its east, then Poland, Belgium, the Netherlands, Norway, and France. The outbreak of the Second World War found England unprepared; at times it seemed that only the inspirational words and unflagging energy of Churchill, who became prime minister in 1940, kept England from capitulating in the face of the relentless bombing attacks visited upon it by Hitler's air force. England endured—experiencing, in the view of Churchill, "its finest hour"—and ultimately prevailed, with the prodigious assistance rendered it by its allies, the United States and the Soviet Union. But again, the cost in human and economic terms was staggering.

In the post–World War II era, England was compelled to dismantle its empire. Most of the former colonies were granted their independence between 1946 and 1980. A commonwealth of 50 nations, all once part

Prime Minister Margaret Thatcher emerges from a British tank during a visit to West Germany in 1986. Thatcher's conservative political program entailed dismantling England's social welfare legislation, privatizing industry, and encouraging individual economic enterprise.

of the empire, is now united only by mutual cooperation; some rely on England for defense. The last remnant of the empire is the six counties of Northern Ireland, which because of its Protestant majority was excluded when Britain agreed to grant otherwise Catholic Ireland its autonomy in 1921. The six counties continue to be under British military occupation, as they have been intermittently for the last 380 years. The Protestant majority there wishes to maintain the political union with England; the Catholic minority continues to resist, sometimes violently, its continued subjugation.

Margaret Thatcher, the nation's first female prime minister, was elected in 1979. Her government has devoted itself to undoing many of the social welfare programs established in England since the Second World War, but Thatcher's restoration of a more classically capitalist economy has not been achieved without considerable controversy. Critics charge that her program has brought a good deal of suffering to the lower classes and the poor and a considerable diminution of civil liberties, but there is no denying that in the 1980s the English economy was much stronger overall than it had been in previous decades. Although Great Britain is today home to just over one percent of the world's population, its economy is the world's sixth largest. The luster of its imperial might is gone, but from its permanent seat on the Security Council of the United Nations (where it is joined by France, China, the United States, and the Soviet Union), Great Britain still commands respect in the international community.

This 17th-century engraving by Theodore de Bry shows Sir Walter Raleigh making peace with the Indians in the New World.

TO PLANT A NATION

The permanent English presence in North America began in May 1607, when 3 ships of the London Company, carrying 104 passengers, among them Captain John Smith, landed at the mouth of the James River in the colony of Virginia. Smith and his men planned to spend the summer trading with the Indians for furs or digging for gold. They expected to make an easy and quick profit both for themselves and for the company that had underwritten their venture.

Thirteen years later, a group of English Puritans who had been in exile in Holland sailed for North America in search of a place where they could live and worship as they chose. After their landing at Plymouth Rock, in what is now Massachusetts, these 100 Pilgrims, as they were called by later generations, established the Plymouth Colony. William Bradford was chosen to be governor; the political and social institutions that were established reflected the Pilgrims' deeply held religious convictions. One critic wrote that a Puritan service was just "four bare walls and a sermon"; the Puritans did away with such vestiges of Catholic ritual that had survived in Church of England worship as stained glass windows, Latin prayers, singing, incense, and the role of the bishop as head of each district. This last element was extremely important. The Puritans believed that religious congregations should govern themselves rather than be governed by a bishop or other figure appointed from above. It was this strain of thought that made England's kings fear them, for they saw correctly that it required only a small intellectual leap to move from belief in self-government in church affairs to self-government in political matters. Indeed, the Puritans were among the most steadfast supporters of Parliament in its struggle with the Crown. Accordingly, in the New World the Puritans established democratic governmental institutions. Even before their landing at Plymouth Rock, the Pilgrims had decided, by virtue of the Mayflower Compact, to govern their colony by majority will.

A popular English ballad inspired by news of the landing in Virginia began, "We hope to build a nation / Where none before hath stood," but as their companions sickened and died during the first New World winter, the surviving colonists in Jamestown, as the Virginia colony was named, must have asked themselves if anything would come from the modest start they had made. The early months in Plymouth were even more difficult; without the assistance of the Indians, the entire colony would most likely have perished. Religion and riches continued to be powerful lures, though, and the two colonies, established for such disparate purposes, succeeded beyond anyone's expectations.

A Fitful Start in Virginia

Jamestown was less than ideally situated. It was located on a peninsula near the mouth of the James River, a swampy region best suited for breeding the mosquitoes that spread malaria. The English adventurers had landed there too late in the year to plant crops, and by spring disease and starvation had killed more than a third. Warmer weather did not bring immediate solace, as the surviving colonists intended to

VIRGINIA

A.D. 1607

JAMES FORTE
AT
JAMES'TOWNE

Powhatan

Discovery

the Susan Constant   *the Gospel*   The River JAMES

John Hull

make a quick fortune, not engage in the backbreaking work of clearing land and planting and sowing crops. Matters improved with the arrival of experienced farmers from England, and the Indians taught the settlers about the use of medicinal herbs for some of the ills that plagued them.

Still, by 1610 the settlers were ready to give up and go home; they were dissuaded only by the arrival of a new governor, Baron De La Warr, who convinced them to try again. The following year, 650 more colonists arrived, but attempts to extract a profit from the New World continued to fail. Glassmaking and mining ventures proved impractical, and agricultural efforts were similarly unsuccessful until the colonists began cultivat-

Initially, the colonists at Jamestown lived inside a triangular fort, seen here in this 17th-century painting. At the upper right is Chief Powhatan, who headed the confederacy of the local tribes. Peace between the Indians and the English was secured for a time by the marriage of the Englishman John Rolfe to Powhatan's daughter, Pocahontas.

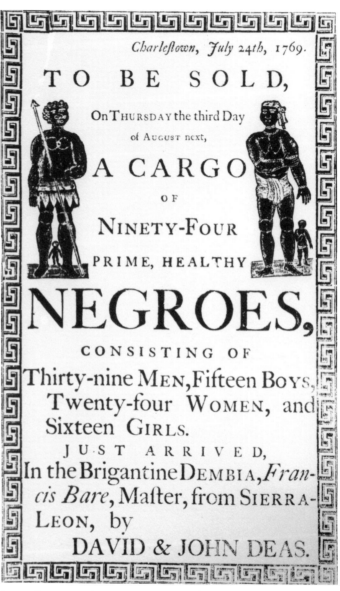

Charleſtown, July 24th, 1769.

TO BE SOLD,

On THURSDAY the third Day
of AUGUST next,

A CARGO

OF

NINETY-FOUR

PRIME, HEALTHY

NEGROES,

CONSISTING OF

Thirty-nine MEN, Fifteen BOYS,
Twenty-four WOMEN, and
Sixteen GIRLS.

JUST ARRIVED,

In the Brigantine DEMBIA, *Francis Bare*, Maſter, from SIERRA-LEON, by

DAVID & JOHN DEAS.

This handbill advertised slaves to be sold in the South Carolina port city of Charlestown (present-day Charleston) on July 24, 1769. The profitable agricultural system established by English colonists in the American South depended on slave labor.

ing tobacco, which Sir Walter Raleigh had noticed the Indians smoking during his 1587 expedition to the New World. By the 1620s, tobacco was the Virginia Colony's most lucrative export, and slave ships had begun to call regularly there in order to sell planters the labor that was needed to cultivate "the weed." The land just north of Virginia, on the Chesapeake Bay, known as Maryland, was granted a royal charter in 1632 under George Calvert, Lord Baltimore, a prominent English Catholic. The colony quickly became a haven for English Catholics and a second center of the tobacco trade. Tobacco would be the New World's most profitable export to England for the next 150 years.

The Puritan Tradition

Plymouth and the other Puritan colony in the New World, Massachusetts Bay, with its center at Boston, endured similar hard times. In the opinion of a visitor from England in the 1620s, Christopher Levett, Massachusetts was a land "good for nothing." The thin, sandy soil and thick pine forests of New England were not ideally suited for agriculture; the New England winters were extremely bitter; and in the first years of the colony, the mortality rate was extremely high. What sustained the Puritans was their unshakable belief in the righteousness of their effort to construct, to quote the metaphor used by John Winthrop, an early governor of the Massachusetts Bay Colony, "a city upon a hill" that would serve as a moral example to the rest of the world. Repression in England continued to drive the Puritans to the New World; 20,000 came in the 1630s alone. This exodus, known as the Great Migration, enabled the establishment of new settlements in Massachusetts and elsewhere. Although many did return to England, particularly following Cromwell's victory in the civil war, those who remained were sustained by a sense of mission described by Francis Higginson, a minister in the colony, as the belief that "if God be with us, who can be against us?"

Most of the Puritan immigrants were artisans or merchants, although some came from poorer circumstances. By and large they hailed from the English counties of Norfolk, Suffolk, and Essex, known collectively as East Anglia and long the bastion of Puritan sentiment. Others came from the west and southwest of England. John Winthrop, who was elected governor of the Massachusetts Bay Colony 12 times between 1630 and 1649, was just one of several remarkable individuals who arrived at the Bay Colony in the 1630s. Among the others were the prominent London merchants Richard Saltonstall and Theophilus Eaton; Anne Hutchinson, a self-taught theologian; and Thomas Dudley, the father of America's first noteworthy poet, Anne Bradstreet.

Towns in New England were laid out like English villages, a fashion that once prevailed in much of America. The meetinghouse, which often served as a

John Winthrop served as governor of the Massachusetts Bay Colony 12 times. The Puritans believed in the theory of predestination, meaning that God singled out at their birth a distinct group of individuals—the elect—for salvation. This theory influenced Winthrop's thoughts about social distinctions, which he believed were divinely ordained. "In all times," he said, "some must be rich, some poor, some high and eminent in power and dignity, others mean and in subjection."

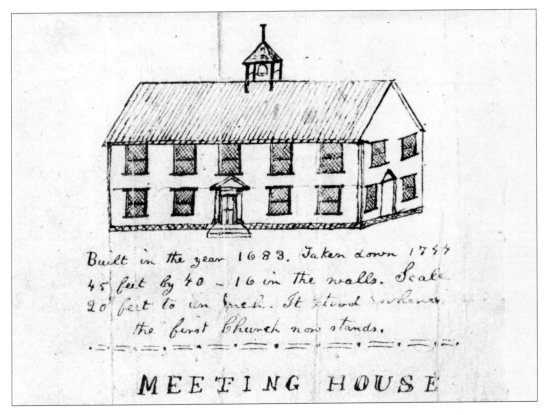

Built in the year 1683. Taken down 1744
45 feet by 40 — 16 in the walls. Scale
20 feet to an inch. It stood where
the first Church now stands.

MEETING HOUSE

kind of town hall as well as a place of worship, and all homes and tradesmen's shops were clustered around the village green, or common, and the land behind was parceled out for farming. Everyone used the surplus common land to graze their animals. Despite the colder climate in New England, houses often had a thatched roof of traditional English design, which failed to provide the needed warmth. Over time, custom gave way to practicality, and brick and stone were found to provide sturdier accommodations. Salem, Boston, Charlestown, Watertown, Lynn, and other towns all arose along similar lines.

The desire to worship freely had driven the Puritans to the New World, but in Massachusetts they were reluctant to extend that same right to others. Roger

The second meetinghouse built in Plymouth served the colony from 1683 to 1744. Such meetinghouses were plain and unadorned, reflecting the Puritan desire to purify the Anglican church of its vestiges of Catholic ritual and pomp.

Williams, a preacher who advocated religious tolerance, was banished from the colony in 1635. He moved on to found the colony of Providence in what would become the colony of Rhode Island. Anne Hutchinson was also exiled for holding the opinion that no minister was needed to interpret God's word to the faithful. Members of the Quaker sect who were made unwelcome in Massachusetts fled to Rhode Island in the 1650s.

A dark corollary to the Puritan belief in God's direct role in human affairs was the notion that behavior and events could be attributed to satanic influences. The Puritan belief in witchcraft culminated in the infamous Salem, Massachusetts, witch trials of 1692. That year, the Puritan elders of Salem put 20 people to death as witches. At right is the frontispiece from an account of the trials written by the influential Puritan minister Increase Mather.

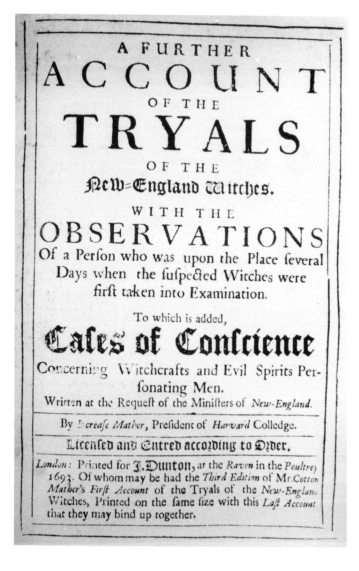

A FURTHER
ACCOUNT
OF THE
TRYALS
OF THE
New-England Witches.
WITH THE
OBSERVATIONS
Of a Person who was upon the Place several
Days when the suspected Witches were
first taken into Examination.

To which is added,
Cases of Conscience
Concerning Witchcrafts and Evil Spirits Per-
sonating Men.
Written at the Request of the Ministers of *New-England*.

By *Increase Mather*, President of *Harvard* Colledge.

Licensed and Entred according to Order.

London: Printed for J. Dunton, at the *Raven* in the *Poultrey*
1693. Of whom may be had the *Third Edition* of Mr. *Cotton*
Mather's First Account of the Tryals of the *New-England*
Witches, Printed on the same size with this *Last Account*
that they may bind up together.

The writings of the influential Puritan minister Cotton Mather, son of Increase Mather, helped inflame the hysteria that led to the Salem witch trials. The younger Mather combined scientific curiosity with his credulous spiritual bent—his advocacy of the newly developed smallpox inoculation is often regarded as the beginning of modern preventive medicine.

Connecticut was first settled by Puritans who would not conform to the strictures of the Massachusetts Bay Colony, and its charter reflected a more tolerant stance. The Massachusetts divines expected complete conformity with their vision of a New Jerusalem, but English immigrants were too independent minded, too energetic, and too self-reliant to be bound for long. (Among the best literary portraits of life in a Puritan community is Nathaniel Hawthorne's novel *The Scarlet Letter*.)

The Bounty of Water and Land

Although at first New England's heavily forested landscape tested the mettle and imagination of its settlers, it soon became apparent that it also offered rare rewards to those willing to work. New England was rich in game, there was land enough for each new settler, the forests offered a seemingly inexhaustible supply of wood, and the profusion of natural harbors and rivers made the region ideally suited for the development of a maritime economy. One settler wrote in 1630, "How serviceable this Country must needs be for provisions for shipping, is sufficiently known already. At present it may yield Planks, Masts, Oares, Pitch, Tarre and Iron, and hereafter . . . if the Colonie increase, Sailes and Cordage."

Next to piety, the Puritans valued industriousness as the highest virtue, and they wasted little time in taking advantage of the blessings that the Lord had provided them. Boston soon became a major commercial hub. Initially, New England's major export was fox, raccoon, and beaver pelts; in exchange, New England tradesmen received tools, salt, housewares, and clothing to sell in the colonies. The sobriety and frugality of New England's merchants soon became well known. England was the most important trading partner, but the colonies also developed independent trade connections with the West Indies.

Independent Thinkers

Economic and political development in the southern colonies took a different course. Tobacco was most profitable when grown on large plantations, an arrangement that was facilitated by the use of slave labor from Africa. The landholding class was smaller than in New England, and the region's most prosperous and powerful individuals were planters rather than merchants. To a large degree, landholders tried to retain the manners, dress, and outlook of the English country gentleman. Pictures from the era show that those who could afford to look and act like an Englishman or Englishwoman did so. A passion for horses, riding, and hunting was part of this ethic.

Because the wealth of Virginia and Maryland was distributed far less evenly than in New England, southern society tended to be less democratic as well. Equally significant was that whereas New England had been settled by dissenters from the Anglican church, in the 17th century Virginia was the only colony in which a majority of the people belonged to the Church of England, with its bishops and hierarchical structure. Southern society also tended to be arranged hierarchically. Plantation owners commanded the most respect and dominated the colony's political and social life; they were deferred to by the less prosperous independent farmer, who was a notch above landless wage laborers and white indentured servants (people who agreed to provide a fixed term of service, usually seven years, in exchange for their passage). At the bottom of the social and economic ladder were the black slaves, but it was their labor that made possible the leisurely, cultivated life enjoyed by the planters. Slave labor and suffering was also the foundation upon which the prosperity of the southern colonies was built. By 1700 there were 8,000 African slaves in Virginia in a total population of 65,000; that number would grow exponentially in the next several decades.

In crucial ways, however, the class system in the southern colonies was much less rigid than in England. The mere availability of as much land as was free to be claimed in the colonies virtually ensured that it would be more fairly distributed than in England. An average farm measured just a few hundred acres, and a smaller percentage of people were landless or indentured than back home. These factors guaranteed a greater degree of social mobility; virtually the only people trapped in a given class were the slaves. In 1663 almost half of the members of the Virginia House of Burgesses, a representative assembly in existence since 1619, were men who had come to the colony as indentured servants. To some observers, the burgesses were a comical mix—a frontiersman in buckskin, hair matted from his woodland labors, sat side by side with a wealthy tobacco planter dressed in silk and sporting a powdered periwig—but the relative absence of entrenched and hereditary privilege, as represented in England by the nobility, made it that much easier for truly democratic institutions to develop. It also made it that much easier to believe in Thomas Jefferson's self-evident truth "that all men are created equal."

The ablest people also tended to rise in New England, where, because most plots of land were a mere 40 to 100 acres, industriousness and diligence were required to farm profitably. Land speculation and royal grants, which led to the creation of huge estates in New York and Virginia, were rare in New England because each township held its land under a common corporation. With their credo of self-reliance and the small size of their farms, the New Englanders had no use for slavery, which meant greater opportunity for wage laborers and prevented the rise of a class of large landholders.

The colonists' move toward establishing a separate, American identity arose out of the need to obtain economic self-determination. Although Virginia, with its Anglican sentiment, might have been expected to maintain closer ties to the Crown than did New England, it was in the South that the first economic unrest arose. When Charles II prevented Virginia planters from selling their tobacco directly to the West Indies or Europe, some plantation owners spoke openly of their dissatisfaction. As the duty required to be paid on tobacco imported to England increased—from 200 percent of the value of the goods in 1660 to 600 percent in 1705—discontent in Virginia became more general. It was in these early conflicts over the tobacco market that the colony became a breeding ground for the men who would eventually govern the American republic.

Intellectual Life

During the time that Cromwell and the parliamentary forces held sway in England, emigration to New

England slowed, in large part because England was now a much more hospitable place for Puritans. Inspired by the Puritan revolution, as the English civil war is sometimes known, many of the English already in Massachusetts returned home. Thomas Hutchinson, an 18th-century governor of Massachusetts, estimated that during the 17th century more English returned home than came to Massachusetts. Gradually, the overtly religious character of the Massachusetts Bay Colony diminished, although the virtues it prized—frugality, practicality, a lack of ostentation—would long be associated with New England. From this increased practical concern with the secular matters of this life would arise the combination of common sense and inventiveness prized as "Yankee ingenuity."

The launching of the first ship built in the American colonies, the Blessing of the Bay, *in 1631.*

This shift can be seen in the life of John Winthrop, Jr. (1606–76). His father was the celebrated governor of the Massachusetts Bay Colony who had presided over a theocracy in which loitering was a crime, maypoles were proscribed as the devil's tools, working on the Sabbath could lead to prison, and blaspheming of a parent by a child was a felony. The younger Winthrop had a less conventional turn of mind, one that prefigured the likes of Benjamin Franklin and Thomas Edison. He lived most of his life in the wilds of upper Connecticut, devoting himself to natural history, his businesses, and correspondence with distant patients about medical cures. He sent rattlesnake skins, bird's nests, plants, and other oddities to the Royal Society (a prominent scientific organization) in London, which responded by making him its first American member. In the words of one historian, he was "struggling to maintain contact with the larger world from which his parents had dared to escape."

But for those in North America with the inclination, such as the younger Winthrop, keeping up-to-date with new ideas and scientific developments could be difficult. Education was conducted mostly at home, the only formal institutions being the Boston Latin School, a grammar school founded in 1635, and Harvard College, founded the next year expressly to train ministers. The college rarely had more than a few dozen students and reached a low point in the last quarter of the 17th century, when it was virtually closed. The well educated also often found greater opportunity back in England—of the nine members of Harvard's first graduating class, seven returned to England. Nevertheless, at the time New England may have had the highest literacy rate in the world, primarily because every family wanted its children to be able to read the Bible. Yale College was founded in New Haven in 1701 by English colonists who found the mind-set in Massachusetts, including its emphasis on religious instruction, somewhat one-dimensional.

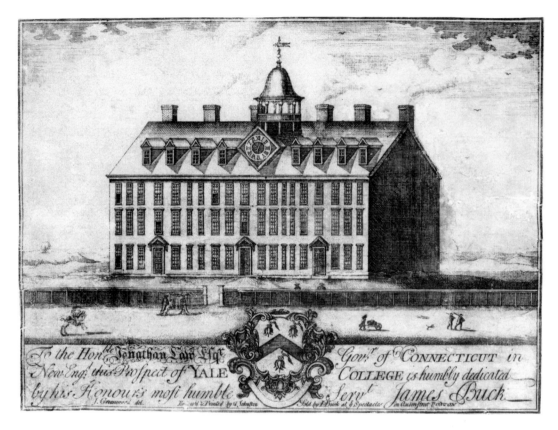

To the Honble Jonathan Law Esqr Govr of CONNECTICUT in New Engd this Prospect of YALE COLLEGE is humbly dedicated by his Honours most humble Servt James Buck

Yale College as it looked in 1749. Now known as Yale University and located in New Haven, Connecticut, the college was founded at Clinton, Connecticut, in 1701. The third-oldest institution of higher learning in the United States, it became in 1861 the first American college to bestow a Ph.D. degree.

Education in the South was less advanced. The populace tended to be spread out across the countryside rather than organized into distinct townships, so for a long time the construction of schools for primary education was unfeasible. The dissemination of information, in the form of books, newspapers, or pamphlets, was poor—the region did not boast a printing press until almost 1700. About half of all Virginians were illiterate. Some of the wealthier parishes could afford to hire a schoolmaster who would travel to see all of his students, just as they had to hire a preacher to come to their churches once a month. (Churches in rural England at the time suffered the same plight.) Where no cash could be found for his services, the itinerant preacher or educator sometimes had to accept tobacco leaves as payment. The first college in the South, William and Mary (named for England's monarchs) was not founded until 1693, and for several decades enrollment there was so low that the school was often in danger of closing.

This is not meant to imply that there were no inquiring minds in the South. William Byrd (1674–1744), a wealthy planter, carried on a wide correspondence and kept a meticulous diary; his writings afford an unparalleled view of colonial Virginia and its unspoiled natural wonders, the intellectual curiosity that the planter class had the leisure to cultivate, and the casual brutality upon which the region's social system was based. In his journals, Byrd praised the taste of polecat and wild turkey, of wild grapes and bear. He describes himself learning which roots to apply to a snakebite, saying his prayers, resting on the Sabbath, and vigorously whipping his slaves. He surveys the land, collects rare flora and fauna, and commits indecencies with female slaves. He describes his library of 3,600 books. Such was the life of a self-styled English country gentleman set loose in the American wilderness.

At the End of the Century

As the 17th century drew to a close, almost 90 percent of the white population of the North American colonies was English by birth or extraction. In both New England and the South, the colonists or their ancestors hailed principally from southern and eastern England. Very few immigrants were rich (the well-off had little reason to leave England) or exceptionally poor (the impoverished generally lacked the means to emigrate). The largest number, by far, were people of middling income or circumstances. The many professionals—such as teachers, clergy, lawyers, doctors, and merchants—were concentrated in New England and New York; artisans and craftsmen, who could make a living anywhere, were spread more evenly throughout the colonies. Indentured servants or former indentured servants accounted for more than half of the total population, but virtually all of them lived in the South. Some "undesirables," such as paupers and criminals, made their way to the New World, almost always as indentured servants. Most of the religions practiced in England were represented in colonial society. Catholics had found a haven in Maryland, Anglicans were predominant in Virginia, Congregationalists (as the Puritans came to be known) in New England, Quakers in Pennsylvania and Rhode Island. Others, including Presbyterians, Baptists, and nonbelievers, lived mainly in the Carolinas or the Middle Atlantic colonies. From this new society, in the next century, would come a new nation.

FROM ENGLISH TO AMERICANS

A new period in the history of the English in North America began in 1689. Following the accession of William and Mary to the British throne, freedom of worship was immediately granted to all Protestants. The guarantee of this right eliminated a major cause of discontent in England, causing emigration to drop for the next 20 years, although it picked up again in the 1720s, 1750s, and 1760s, amid the brief periods of peace that broke out during the almost constant European warfare of the period. The typical English immigrant of the 18th century was of a slightly lower social and economic class than his predecessors of the preceding century, and he was less likely to possess religious convictions. No longer did he share North America almost exclusively with his countrymen, either, for in the 18th century large numbers of French, German, Scotch, and Scotch-Irish immigrants also began to settle in the 13 colonies and Canada. The influx of these newcomers was particularly notable in the Middle Atlantic colonies, especially Pennsylvania.

Remaking Rural England

Yet newcomers from England would still have recognized much that was familiar. Farming practices, for one, were similar in many regards to those used in England since the Middle Ages. Farmers cleared land using time-honored English methods—either by stripping trees of their bark, then burning around the roots, or "girdling" the tree (chopping around its base and leaving it to die).

Over time, farmers in the New World developed new methods and learned to grow new crops. In New England, the grain that Americans called corn was particularly favored, as it could be cultivated by hand, demanding less equipment and labor. With pork and fish, corn became a staple of the New Englander's diet. Wheat, a more versatile grain well known to the English, was grown in the fertile reaches between the Hudson and the Potomac rivers, America's first breadbasket. Farther south, in South Carolina, the important cash crops were indigo and rice, neither of which were grown in England.

The agricultural wealth of the colonies found a lucrative market in the British colonies in the West Indies, which English immigrants had settled at about the same time as the 13 colonies. Virtually all of the arable land in the West Indies was devoted to producing sugarcane (as in the American South, large plantations worked by slaves were the norm), which meant that the islands imported much of their food items and building materials from North America—beef, fish, pigs, lumber, nails, flour, and vegetables. But the most important American agricultural products were two nonfood crops, tobacco and cotton. Needed as the raw material for England's proliferating textile mills once the Industrial Revolution was under way, cotton would supplant tobacco as the most profitable southern export. It

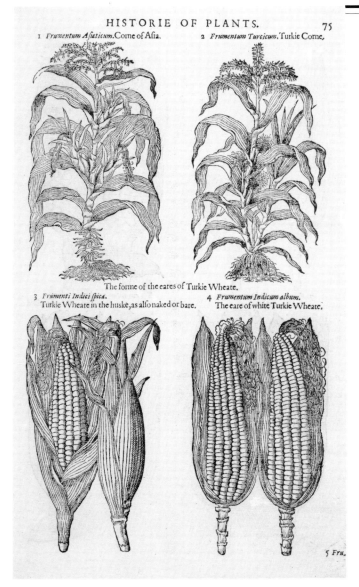

1 *Frumentum Afiaticum.*Corne of Afia.   2 *Frumentum Turcicum.*Turkie Corne.

The forme of the eares of Turkie Wheate.

3 *Frumenti Indici fpica.*   4 *Frumentum Indicum album.*
Turkie Wheate in the huske, as alfo naked or bare.   The eare of white Turkie Wheate.

5 *Fru.*

An engraving of corn from a book published in 1597 in England, The Herbal. *English settlers in the New World learned how to grow corn from the Indians, and in New England it soon became a staple of the settlers' diet.*

would also become the basis for a southern way of life increasingly dependent upon slavery. In the early 18th century, slaves constituted half of the South's population. Landowners in the South were most commonly of English ancestry, but not necessarily English-American: In 1703 most of the 3,500 free whites in South Carolina had migrated from the English colony of Barbados.

The "Desperate Villaines"

There was also a class of white immigrant that came to the colonies involuntarily. Between 1607 and the outbreak of the American Revolution in 1775, approximately 50,000 English criminals were transported to the colonies (most to Virginia and Maryland), where the rights to their labor for the duration of their sentence were purchased by landowners or merchants. Many returned home when their term was up; many more stayed. An estimated 20,000 were present in 1776, building or repairing roads, working the fields, or escaping west. One study has revealed that few were hardened criminals: The most frequent offense was stealing sheep or horses.

Punishment of criminal behavior in the colonies, particularly in Puritan New England, included confinement in the stocks, a wooden frame with openings in it in which the feet or hands could be locked. Humiliation was part of the punishment; the offender was usually confined out of doors in a public area.

ELIZABETH CANNING,
Drawn from the Life, as fhe ftood at the Bar to receive her Sentence, in the
Seffion's-Houfe, in the *Old-Bailey*.

Convicted of perjury in 1754, Elizabeth Canning receives the court's sentence—one month in jail and "Transportation for seven Years, to one of his Majesty's Colonies in America." The sentences of many English convicts included indentured servitude in the American colonies.

The presence of convicts, whatever their offense, vexed many a colonist. In 1670 the Virginia Assembly tried to ban "fellons and other desperate villaines sent hither from the several prisons of England." Maryland followed suit six years later. Both laws remained on the books until 1718, and most of the colonies passed a similar law at one time or another, only to have it vetoed by Parliament. British courts continued to sentence convicts to transportation overseas until the Revolution, and one colony, Georgia, which received a royal charter in 1732, was even conceived as a rehabilitation project for the denizens of England's notorious debtor's prisons. Convicts were so prevalent in the colonies that Benjamin Franklin even filed a half-jesting "Petition to Swap Rattlesnakes for Convicts," but like other immigrants of the English lower classes, convicts were sometimes able to benefit from the greater social

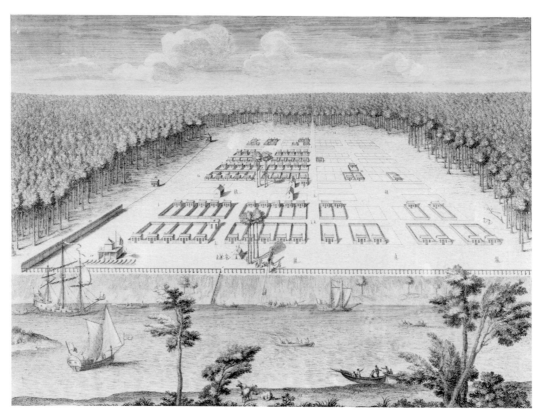

An artist's view of Savannah, Georgia, in 1734. The colony of Georgia had been founded a year earlier by James Edward Oglethorpe, a wealthy English philanthropist, who conceived of it as a place where those who had been confined to debtor's prison in England could make a new start.

mobility at work in America. Anthony Lamb, accomplice to a notorious English thief, served his sentence in Virginia, then moved to Philadelphia and became a manufacturer of mathematical instruments. His son John was a successful merchant and became a general in the Continental Army during the Revolution.

The large number of convicts and other individuals from the lower strata of British society may have contributed to the rough-edged, violent quality of daily life that so many observers of colonial society commented on. In the South, a convicted thief might have his eye gouged out or an ear cropped. Fistfighting, either for honor or for sport, was common among the rural folk; plantation owners preferred to settle their differences with swords or pistols. Dueling was not unheard of among the upper classes. Harsh treatment of convicts and indentured servants, including physical punishment, was commonplace. According to one historian, "the status of the transported convict, while legally akin to that of the voluntary servant, tended in practice to be closer to that of the [black] slave, and may at times have been worse."

The prevalence of violence in southern life is perhaps not so surprising given the brutality inherent in the slave system, upon which the South's economy depended. That brutality was, for the most part, a given (and accepted) hallmark of southern society. A member of the Stafford family, who fled debts in England for Carolina in 1711, wrote that one could "get a few slaves and can beat them well to make them work hard. There is no living here without."

The Role of Women

Englishwomen in the colonies were resourceful and resilient. Survival in a newly established wilderness community required the cooperation of all its members, and women seldom found their responsibilities limited to the kitchen and home. Many frontierswomen knew how to handle a gun, and in New Hampshire in 1697 women were offered £50 for each Indian scalp they collected. More typical of a woman's duties, however, was her responsibility for clothing her family. Three-quarters of the clothing worn by colonists was made of homespun, rough but practical cloth turned out in households across the land. Women performed most of this work.

The unsettled nature of colonial American society provided women with a good deal of opportunity that might not have been available to them at home. Sarah Kemble Knight, for example, was born in Boston in 1666 to English immigrants. Her husband, a ship captain, died young, so she quickly taught herself some law; she also ran a school, a shop, and a boardinghouse, making a success of all and leaving a handsome estate. The Puritan strain is evident in her vigor, her practicality,

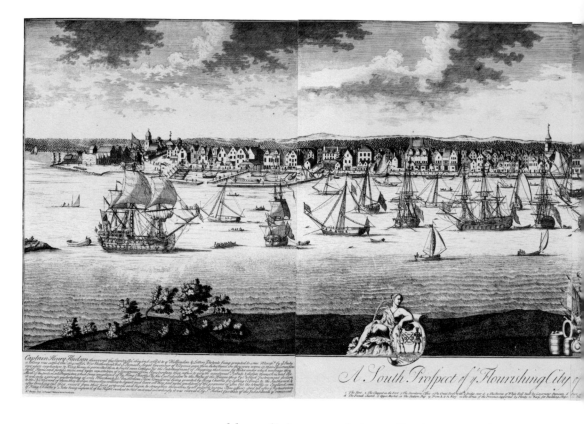

Captain Henry Hudson discovered this Countrie &c. [remainder of engraving text illegible]

A South Prospect of y.ᵉ Flourishing City of

and her religious convictions. During a trip she made to New York City in 1704 she noted disapprovingly in her journal, "They are not strict in keeping the Sabbath as in Boston and other places." Other entries provide a glimpse at the details of colonial life; upon visiting a fine house, she noted that "the hearths were laid with the finest tile that I ever see, and the stair cases laid all with white tile which is ever clean, and so are the walls of the Kitchen which had a brick floor."

Marriage in the colonies was often as much a matter of practical necessity as it was a matter of the heart, particularly in the hinterlands. Unmarried women were a rarity, in large part because a wife's economic value as a cook, weaver, farmhand, and all her other myriad roles was so high. As early as 1666, one observer commented that if Englishwomen in the colonies were "civil and under 50 years of age, some honest man or

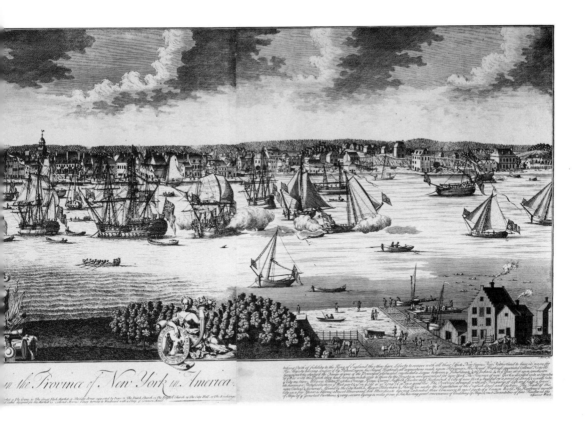

in the Province of New York in America.

other will purchase them." English novelist and journalist Daniel Defoe observed in 1725 that "there were so many Women more than Men that sold themselves to go over to Virginia, and our other Plantations in America, that I should find it was equal to all the great numbers of men who went away in time of War."

An engraving by the artist William Burgis of a view of New York City from the south in the early 18th century. New York was shaped by its dual English and Dutch legacy.

New York: An Exceptional Colony

In many ways, New York was always an exception among the colonies. Its Dutch origins made it singular, as did the diverse ethnic composition of its populace. (England won the colony, then called New Amsterdam, from the Netherlands in 1664. It was renamed after the duke of York, the future James II.) By the mid-17th century, 18 different languages were being spoken on the island of Manhattan. In New York City, located at the mouth of the Hudson River, English Protestants, Catholics, Huguenots, and Jews all worshiped within a few square miles of one another. By 1776, New York City was a thriving commercial center; home to 20,000 people, it had overtaken Boston as the second-largest colonial city, behind Philadelphia.

The English influence in New York City, although relatively small in comparison with other places, was significant. A Swedish visitor observed in 1748 that "most of the young people now speak principally *English*, and go only to the *English* church; and would even take it amiss, if they were called *Dutchmen* and not *Englishmen*." Sarah Kemble Knight observed the difference between the English and the Dutch as a matter of sartorial taste: "The English go very fashionable in their dress. But the Dutch . . . differ from our women, in their habitt go loose, wear French [caps], leaving their ears bare, which are sett out with Jewells of a large size and many in number." New York was also the only bastion of the Church of England north of the Potomac River, and during the Revolution it was home to more Loyalists than any other northern colony.

New Blood

With its defeat of France in the Seven Years' War, England solidified its control of North America. France was forced to relinquish its claims to Canada and all lands east of the Mississippi, except New Orleans. Peace brought with it a new wave of immigration from England. Between 1760 and 1775, about 30,000 English came to North America. This migration was so significant that in 1773 Parliament considered banning immigration to North America. Although convinced not to do so by the lobbying of merchants and pamphleteers on both sides of the Atlantic, including Benjamin Franklin, Parliament did commission the gathering of comprehensive information about the emigrants. Customs officials were required to record

(continued on page 81)

BECOMING AMERICANS

Overleaf: The Mayflower at anchor off Plymouth, Massachusetts, 1621. The ship that carried the Pilgrims to the New World also served as their first home there while they constructed homes ashore. Many 18th-century artists captured different aspects of the life of English colonists in America. At right is a portrait of Captain Samuel Chandler by Winthrop Chandler; below is the family of Boston merchant Isaac Royall.

In the mid-18th century, Boston was the most important city in New England and the birthplace of much of the unrest that would culminate in the American Revolution. The building at the center of this painting is the Old State House, from where the officials of the British colonial government ruled.

William Penn, the founder of Pennsylvania, concluded a treaty with the Indians in 1682 that helped ensure a harmonious beginning for the colony. Below is the intersection of Second and High streets in Philadelphia, the city that became the first capital of the United States in 1777; at the time it was the second largest English-speaking city in the world.

The family of John Cadwalader, a prominent Philadelphian of the late 18th century, as painted by Charles Willson Peale, America's foremost portraitist of the period.

Soldier, courtier, explorer, and poet, Sir Walter Raleigh (above) organized the expedition that established the first English colony in America, off the coast of North Carolina in 1585. The South is still home to a high concentration of people of English descent.

The fox hunt was just one pleasure of English country life that southern planters sought to emulate (below). At left, the trustees of the colony of Georgia welcome representatives of Indian tribes to a peace conference. Georgia was conceived as a colony where the denizens of England's debtor's prisons could make a fresh start; initially, both slavery and rum were prohibited there.

A crowd of patriots pulls down the statue of England's king George III in New York City in 1776. The Declaration of Independence, which was proclaimed in January of that year, announced that the Americans were ready to sever their political ties with the motherland.

(continued from page 72)

the "name, age, quality, occupation, employment, & former residence" of each passenger bound for America.

The results of this survey show that almost half of those departing were under the age of 25. Three-quarters were male, although of those who had been living in London, that figure was 90 percent. Half were indentured servants or otherwise bound; the next-largest category was artisans. About one-third of the emigrants were traveling with family; of these, the majority came from the north of England. They arrived in America during a period of economic growth—North Carolina, Delaware, and New Jersey, in particular, were developing rapidly—and great political unrest.

Maturity and "Great Solidity"

On one level, taxation was the immediate cause of the American Revolution, which sundered permanently the political ties that joined the 13 colonies and England. The cost to England of defending its North American empire in the French and Indian War (as the North American theater of the Seven Years' War was known) had been enormous; the king, George III, and Parliament believed it only reasonable that the English subjects in the colonies should undertake to pay for some of the cost of that defense, which protected their interests as well as the Crown's. They proposed that the colonists do so through the payment of taxes; the colonists replied that they already did so through their payment of the various duties that England levied on exports and imports. When England responded by imposing a series of revenue-raising measures — the Sugar Act and the Stamp Act, among others—colonial opposition was fierce. England's long history of opposition to lawless monarchy had made its people extremely sensitive to the issue of unjust taxation, and it was in this tradition that many of the colonial opponents of the measures believed they were acting.

The colonists recognized England's right to control trade by virtue of customs regulations—although a good deal of energy was devoted to circumventing trade rules—but they believed that revenue-raising measures in the form of direct taxes could only be imposed by legislative bodies in which they were directly represented, namely, their own colonial legislatures rather than Parliament. Direct representation, the colonists believed, was a right that all English had earned by virtue of their ancestors' opposition to tyrannical monarchs. The English government's announcement that violators of the Stamp Act would be tried in special courts, without benefit of a jury of their peers, further convinced the colonists that their democratic rights were being trampled upon.

On another level, it can be argued that the American Revolution was the inevitable upshot of the economic development that made it necessary for the colonies to obtain their independence. By July 4, 1776, when independence was declared, the colonies were exceedingly prosperous. Grain and vegetables were plentiful. The New England whaling fleet numbered 300 ships, and British fishermen were complaining to Parliament that the colonists took the prize of the North Atlantic catch. American artisans and shopkeepers no longer had to depend on European materials or styles. By the late 17th century, colonial hatmakers, for example, were working beaver pelts (once a prime export) into the headgear and clothing accessories that were then so fashionable. Paul Revere, a homegrown Renaissance man, crafted some of the finest silver objets d'art of the age and also won renown as an engraver of prints. Pipemakers used their excess clay to fabricate curling pegs for wigs and other useful implements. For cabinetmakers, America's walnut, cherry, and maple trees yielded the stuff of some of the century's loveliest furniture.

America's economic development gave it a certain power to defy the British government, for England needed America's raw materials and its people's ingenuity. Philadelphia had grown into one of the largest

cities in the British Empire, with 40,000 residents churning out household goods, ironware, and tools every bit the equal of the efforts of European craftsmen. Pennsylvania and the other middle colonies, in fact, had more furnaces and forges blazing in 1775 than all of industrialized England and Wales combined. A goodly number of London's and Bristol's merchants owed their livelihood to tobacco, cotton, and indigo imported from the American South. In all, one-seventh of the kingdom's trade came from its North American colonies. It is little wonder that the colonists came to believe that any interference with their economic activity, without their consent, was unwarranted.

1775: England and the English Divided

It is important to remember that when war broke out between Great Britain and the 13 American colonies in April 1775, each colony generally still had closer links

This engraving illustrating one of the proverbs penned by Benjamin Franklin in his popular Poor Richard's Almanack *was done by Paul Revere. One of the most talented artisans in the colonies, Revere earned his greatest fame for his midnight ride at the outset of the American Revolution, when he rode from Boston to Lexington and Concord to warn the minutemen that the British were coming.*

A British Loyalist, or Tory, is hoisted by the seat of his pants by an irate crowd of American patriots during the American Revolution. Other Tories were tarred and feathered and even had their homes and businesses burned.

to London than it did to its neighbors. The type of colonial government in each varied, as did their conception of what they hoped to gain from the war. The populace of each varied, too. The four New England colonies were predominantly English, although many of their residents were by this point fourth- and fifth-generation Americans. The five southern colonies were also largely British (less so English, meaning that they were also inhabited by a significant number of Scotch, Scotch-Irish, and Welsh). The four middle colonies were the most mixed—only 30 percent of New Yorkers were English by ancestry, for example—although they were generally English in custom and language.

That these ties with England were highly regarded is indicated by the vigorous opposition in the colonies to the war. "Our invaluable charter," wrote one colonist, "secures to us all English Liberties. . . . Happy, beyond Expression! in the Form of our Government—In the Liberty we enjoy." John Adams estimated that one-third of the colonists supported the rebellion, one-third were Loyalists, and one-third were neutral. Of the English who had arrived since 1763, a slight majority, especially among the well-to-do, remained loyal (or later said they had when asking Parliament to reimburse them for property losses). Seventy regiments of Loyalists—as many as 50,000 colonists—fought alongside the British redcoats. At the same time, even some English recognized the great gulf that now separated Englishmen and Americans. In 1770 a London newspaper reported that the king's governors were "generally entire Strangers to the People they are sent to govern."

Further evidence that both sides still felt the pull of their common birthright, language, and heritage may be seen in the way that the war was conducted. Many English soldiers refused to take up arms against their "American cousins," and their places had to be taken by Scots and by German mercenaries. British officers later observed that the war was less barbaric than most and that the men in their command behaved better toward the colonists, both civilians and combatants, than they usually did toward their enemies in European wars. Some historians consider the American Revolution to have been a sort of civil war in which English subjects fought one another to determine whether a new form of English civilization would take root. The colonists won, and the English in America became English Americans.

POURING OUT TO AMERICA IN THOUSANDS

The words above were written by an English immigrant in 1834 to describe the migration of families from his homeland to America. In 1790 the first census of the United States of America counted 3.9 million residents, including slaves. Approximately 1.93 million of these—about 60 percent of the white population—were of English ancestry. About 40,000 had been born in England. Over the next 130 years, more than 3.5 million English would come to America.

Dreamers and Doers

In the aftermath of the American Revolution, the English in the United States had to define their political loyalties. Those who were unsympathetic to the new republic and its democratic ideals or who simply found it too difficult to end a lifetime of loyalty to England returned home. During the revolutionary war and immediately afterward, approximately 100,000 English— 1 out of every 25 members of society—left the United States.

Those who stayed were often among the most enthusiastic supporters of America's democratic experiment. One such Englishman was George Courtauld, who in 1785 sold his silk mill in order to buy a farm in New York. However, Courtauld devoted more of his energies to the fight to get the Constitution ratified in New York than he did to his crops, and he wound up deeply in debt. He was forced to give up his farm and return to England, but his commitment to the United States remained steadfast, and he later resettled in Ohio.

America had always been a haven for English unsatisfied with the political situation at home; with the success of the colonies in their battle for independence, the new nation became that much more attractive to those of an antimonarchical or republican bent. Around the world as well, the American Revolution was seen as an inspirational blow in the battle against oppressive tyranny, and nowhere more so than in France, where the French Revolution, which unseated King Louis XVI, began in 1789. Europe's monarchs were naturally made uneasy by the republican sentiment unleashed by the two revolutions, and those English who were too outspoken in their support for the French Revolution found themselves the target of government persecution. Thousands came to the United States in the 1790s. In an America that seemed to be alive with democratic opportunity, some tried to put their political ideals into practice through the establishment of utopian communities. Most of these ventures did not last long; the story of one such effort in Illinois is illustrative.

The idea for the community was suggested by Ninian Edwards, Illinois's first territorial governor, to Morris Birkbeck, a high-minded English Quaker opponent of slavery who was looking for land and the freedom to practice his political and religious beliefs. In 1816, Birkbeck commissioned a friend, George Flower, to purchase 16,000 acres located on a plain near the Wabash River in Edwards County, Illinois. There, Birkbeck and Flower founded two towns, Albion and

Wanborough, although locals called the site English Prairie. In no time the settlements held between them 45 cabins, 2 taverns, a church, a market house, a library, many shops and stores, a cooper, a bricklayer, 2 black-smiths, and several carpenters. Albion was home to 60 English families totaling 400 people, and Wanborough's population was even higher. Pitching in as needed were the people of New Harmony, Indiana, a utopian community founded at the same time on the other side of the Wabash by the Welsh-born philanthropist Robert Owen.

A series of promotional letters written by George Flower's son Richard and published in London informed would-be immigrants about the venture. Richard Flower mentioned the 700 Americans living in Albion, "who like the English for their neighbors, and many of whom are good neighbors to us." He also approved of the American people's "love of civil and religious liberty [which] is unbounded in every Illinois heart," but he was realistic about certain drawbacks:

George Flower and his wife helped found the utopian settlements of Albion and Wanborough near the Wabash River in Illinois. Both were populated mainly by English immigrants. Their son Richard wrote letters promoting the project that were published in Britain.

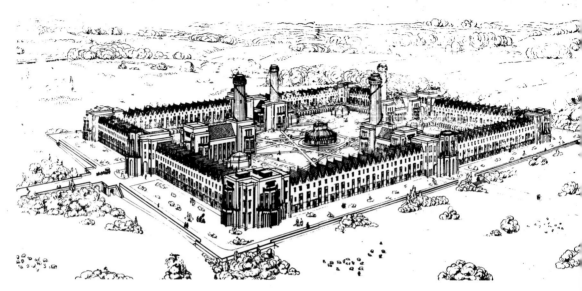

Robert Owen's socialist convictions led to the founding of New Harmony, Indiana, which he conceived as a community that would provide for the education and welfare of its inhabitants. Seen here is an architect's drawing of Owen's elaborate design for New Harmony.

"Some who have emigrated to America find themselves as unhappy there as they were in their own country. Those . . . whose minds are rivetted to the artificial distinctions of society in Europe, have found to their cost, that America is not the country for them."

Unfortunately, it appears that some of Albion's and Wanborough's settlers might have included Morris Birkbeck among those ill at ease with the relative absence of social and class distinctions that then characterized American society. Initially active in the campaign for Illinois statehood, he later gave up the Quaker faith and began preaching a Church of England service in Wanborough. Many settlers considered him haughty and called him behind his back the Emperor of the Prairie, and he was ridiculed for his efforts to construct a luxurious manor house for himself.

Of even greater import to the well-being of Birkbeck's settlements was that the location of Wanborough left it without access to well water. The soil was poor, and Wanborough folded within a decade of its founding. Birkbeck drowned in 1825 while crossing a stream to visit Robert Owen, and his wife and four children left Illinois the same year. Some of the settlers, disheartened, returned to England, but most (including George Flower) stayed on or moved to neighboring towns.

In 1900 a few of the original settlers were among the town's 1,162 residents. One of them, who had been a little girl at the time, recalled the sights and sounds of a cricket match in progress on the prairie and how the English had eventually intermarried with their Dutch, French, and American neighbors.

One of a multitude of farm towns founded in the Midwest by the English, Albion survives to this day.

Getting Rich, or Lonely

America's own transportation revolution opened the trans-Appalachian territories to a land rush in the 1820s and 1830s. The British government's attempts to restrict settlement west of the Appalachians had been one of many points of dispute with the colonists, but in the early decades of the 19th century Americans hastily constructed roads, bridges, and canals that enabled them to move west. The first railroad line to slice through the mountains connected Baltimore with Ohio in 1829. An Englishman wrote then, "The whole continent presents a scene of *scrambling* and roars with greedy hurry. Go ahead! is the order of the day."

The English were among the thousands of immigrants who began pouring into Ohio, Illinois, Wisconsin, Michigan, and Iowa in search of both land and, as one put it, "independence from all supercilious and brow-beating superiors." At two dollars per acre, land in the 1840s was enticing to those who found England's factory towns less and less appealing. But the English were not alone in their rush for the open spaces of the West. New immigrants, chief among them the Germans and Scandinavians, were also moving west in large numbers, and it was no longer possible to think of

English-born David Hilton, his family, and some of their livestock were photographed on the Nebraska prairie in 1889. The family is seated around a player piano; even on the lonesome prairies English immigrants sought to maintain their cultural traditions.

America as an extension of England. The changes made many English ill at ease. "The English tongue is practically all that is English in America," wrote William Oliver from Illinois. From Ohio, another Englishman wrote of the "many homesick complaining English folk in this country." Yet it was undeniable that compared to the majority of other immigrants from northern and western Europe who were entering America at the time,

Ebenezer Beesley, a Mormon from Oxfordshire, England, moved to Salt Lake City, Utah, when the hand-cart company that employed him relocated. He eventually became the musical director of the famous Mormon Tabernacle Choir.

the English fit in much more readily, if only by virtue of the language they shared with Americans. One indication of this ease of adjustment is that it was more common for English immigrants to marry native-born Americans than it was for immigrants from any other ethnic group.

In some regards, however, the English Americans clung to the familiar things of home. Although it is generally true that for the new generation of English immigrants, economic rather than religious considerations were the primary motive for immigration, "finding an opportunity to attend religious services was as important to most of them as finding English friends," according to a modern historian, Charlotte Erickson. Shakers started towns in New England; Methodists and Episcopalians (as Anglicans are known in the United States) built churches everywhere; and English-born Mormons made Salt Lake City, Utah, the most English city in the country by late century.

American Industry, English Labor

Industrial competition was one spur to the new English immigration. With the Industrial Revolution well under way in Britain, artisans, craftsmen, and other workers—such as hand-loom operators—who had been displaced by the changes in British society went to ply their craft in the United States, where there was still a demand for their services. Known as the father of of American manufacturing, Samuel Slater left Manchester, England, in disguise in 1789 with plans for the construction of a cotton-spinning machine. Over the next 15 years, he built the first spinning mills in America. Workers with certain skills, including engineers and technicians on the cutting edge of the iron, steel, textile, and pottery industries, were officially prohibited from emigrating, but U.S. firms recruited them openly nevertheless.

Although many of the new English immigrants were attracted by the land and freedom to be found in the Midwest, the great majority settled on the eastern seaboard, particularly in the Northeast. Pennsylvania and New Jersey were especially popular. From 1640 until the revolutionary war, the South had displaced the Northeast as the most common destination of English immigrants, but the slave states would never again be so favored by immigrants of any nation, simply because it was impossible for them to compete economically with slave labor. The one southern region that was an

WINDING ROOM, LANCASHIRE COTTON MILL. 62174 J.V.

exception was Texas, a magnet for English settlers in the 1830s and 1840s. About one-fifth of the 180 men who died in defense of the Alamo in 1836, during the Texans' struggle for independence from Mexico, were born in England.

Some 600,000 English immigrants came to the United States in the four score and five years between the outbreak of the American Revolution and the Civil War. At times, it seemed that entire industries were being transplanted nearly intact from England to America. This trend was particularly noticeable with regard to

The winding room of a cotton mill in Lancashire, England, in the early 20th century. The American textile industry recruited many skilled workers from England.

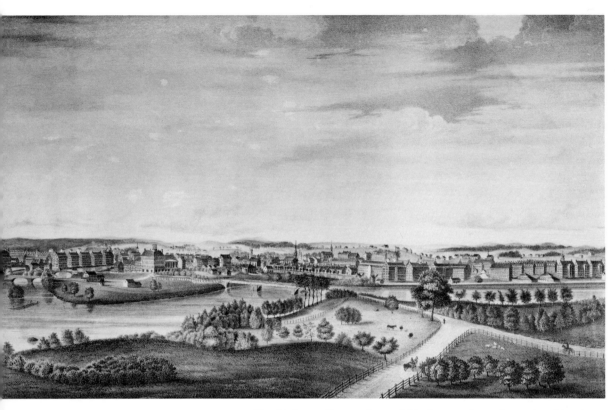

A view of Lowell, Massachusetts, in about 1833. One of America's major textile manufacturing cities in the 19th century, Lowell employed many transplanted British workers.

English textile workers. Woolen makers from Bradford, England, immigrated to Lawrence, Massachusetts, in such profusion that it was dubbed the Bradford of America, and a newspaper in the town was called the *Anglo-American*. England's cotton-spinning industry, with one base in the Lancashire city of Bolton, lost thousands of its workers to the new mills in the Massachusetts cities of Fall River and New Bedford. One ship captain said about the Lancashire emigrants he carried across the ocean, "When they reach Newfoundland or about there, the first question they ask is, 'Where is Fall River?'" A section of another Massachusetts town, Lowell, was dubbed English Row after the immigrants who settled there. Carpet weavers from the English city of Kidderminster began immigrating to Philadelphia in large numbers in 1815; 70 years later,

6,000 English, most of them from Kidderminster, worked in Philadelphia's many carpet works.

Similar examples are legion. Cutlery makers from Sheffield congregated in Waterbury, Connecticut. After the American Civil War, workers from England's silk industry moved to the United States virtually en masse; more than 15,000 silk workers from Macclesfield and Coventry left England to staff the new mills being established in Paterson, New Jersey, where much of the work was done by family-run concerns still reliant on hand-loom operators. Lace makers began leaving Nottingham for Brooklyn, New York, and other sites in 1883. Knitters in the hosiery business, centered in Leicester and Nottingham, began leaving for Philadelphia in the 1830s. At the time it was sometimes the practice for a factory owner to take his entire staff along when shifting sites, even across the ocean; when the hosiery industry gravitated toward Needham, Massachusetts, 20 years later, its workers followed. There were English potters in East Liverpool, Ohio, and Trenton, New Jersey; iron-workers in Troy, New York; miners in Illinois; steel-workers in Pittsburgh; printers in Boston and Chicago; carpenters and builders seemingly everywhere.

English capital as well as English labor benefited American industry, as it helped launch in the United States virtually every imaginable industrial venture. Transplanted English and Scots owned and managed a large share of the American textile industry; many of them became naturalized citizens. American capitalists learned from their English counterparts. Francis Cabot Lowell, scion of one of Boston's oldest families, went to Lancashire, England, in 1810–12 to observe the operation of the mills there. Upon his return, he directed the installation of America's first cotton mill, at Fall River. At nearby Waltham, he built a complete mill where spinning and weaving could be conducted under one roof.

American capitalists also learned how to extract maximum productivity from the work force. In the

A set of illustrations from 1866 depicting the stages of immigration, from departure to arrival and processing at Castle Garden, the primary point of entry for immigrants during the first great wave of European immigration.

early decades of the 19th century, hourly wages in America for cotton spinners, for example, were 3 to 4 times higher than they were in England, but until 1874 the typical worker labored 11 hours a day for 6 days a week. American mills also used cotton of poorer quality, making the spinning more difficult. In the latter part of the century, during the second great wave of European immigration, the number of potential workers exceeded the number of available jobs, and wages plummeted to below what they were in England. Long hours and little pay moved one English-American worker to think fondly of home. "What, call this a free land and ask a mon to slave in such a fashion! Here's back t'owd England," he wrote. Many immigrants did return home, either because they were dissatisfied or because they had done in America what they had set out to do — earn enough money to make a new start in England. On the whole, however, English workers fared better than other immigrants, particularly those from eastern and southern Europe, simply because their language skills and their "familiarity" to Americans made them relatively unlikely to be subjected to the discrimination and prejudice that other immigrants faced.

The landing of the United Empire Loyalists, American colonists who had remained loyal to England, at Saint John, New Brunswick, in 1783.

THE ENGLISH CANADIANS

Unlike the Americans, the Canadians fought no war for independence. When, seeking unity and greater control over their internal affairs, Canada's four original provinces petitioned Britain for self-rule, the English government granted them autonomy. The Canadians, in turn, took many of the principles of the British system of government and applied them to their own rule.

At the time of Canada's federation in 1867, three of its provinces—Ontario, New Brunswick, and Nova Scotia—were peopled predominantly by those of English descent. The fourth, Quebec, was heavily French. That demographic trend reflected the pattern of Canada's original settlement and has persisted to the present day. A little more than 100 years before Canada's federation, during the French and Indian War, Britain and France had clashed over which of them was to rule Canada. Although in the late 19th century Canadian society began to grow increasingly multiethnic as the result of the same wave of European immigration that brought so many newcomers to the United States — today it is composed of people from more than two dozen cultures — the long conflict between the English and the French over cultural, linguistic, and political matters has continued throughout Canadian history. This long-standing rivalry has served to make English Canadians even more aware and proud of their ancestry.

Gaining a Foothold

English claims to Canada began with the "discovery" of Newfoundland by the explorer John Cabot in 1497. (The region, of course, was already inhabited by

This portrait of King Charles II graced the royal charter granted the Hudson's Bay Company in 1670. By the 1830s, the company enjoyed a virtual monopoly on the Canadian fur trade and governed a huge expanse of Canadian territory that stretched from the Atlantic to the Pacific.

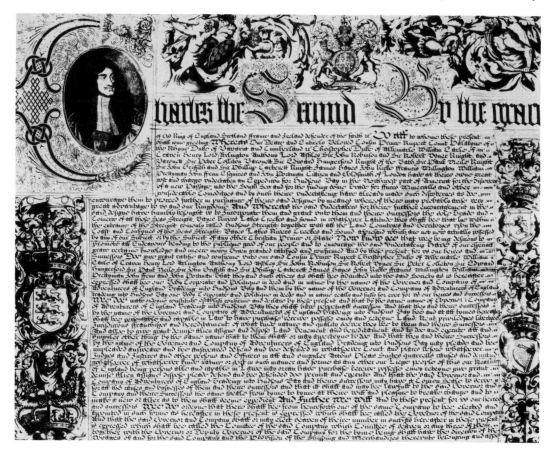

Indians.) French claims dated from the explorations of Jacques Cartier, who reached the mouth of the St. Lawrence River in 1534. The 1610 expedition of Henry Hudson gave England claim to the great bay that bears his name and to the regions surrounding it, but initially it was French explorers, fur trappers, and missionaries who took the lead in exploring the Canadian interior as far west as the Great Lakes. The French were also more active in establishing permanent settlements. But by the 1670s, the English, attracted by the great wealth of furs to be extracted from Canada's forests, had taken a greater interest in the region, and trappers from the Hudson's Bay Company roamed the continent from the Atlantic to the Pacific. The number of English immigrants in Canada grew. By terms of a peace treaty

The Woolsey family were successful merchants in Lower Canada in the early 19th century. As English, they were in the minority in Lower Canada, which was one of two colonies into which the English government had divided Quebec. Government in Upper Canada, where the English were the majority, was based on English law; government in Lower Canada, where the French predominated, was based on French models.

On October 13, 1812, a U.S. invasion force of 600 men crossed the Niagara River into Canada and attempted to take Queenston Heights. Their initial assault was successful, but they were soon forced to withdraw by a larger British force.

that France, defeated in European wars, was compelled to sign in 1713, it surrendered to Britain its claims to the Canadian regions of Newfoundland, Acadia (renamed Nova Scotia), and the Hudson Bay region. Although still outnumbered by the French in Canada, the English in all of North America now outnumbered the French by more than 20 to 1. Fifty years later, England's victory in the French and Indian War virtually eliminated France as a political power from North America.

English from Far and Near

Britain's victory stimulated further English settlement in Canada, particularly in its eastern regions. After the American Revolution, some 40,000 to 60,000 Loyalists to the British crown sought refuge in Canada. At least half of these newcomers were born in England; virtually all of the rest were of English descent. Most were of the middle class—Anglican churchmen and their families, government officials, a few English Catholics, property owners or merchants. About 30,000 of the United Empire Loyalists, as they were known, moved to the Atlantic seaboard; 14,000 of them flocked to Saint John, New Brunswick, then part of Nova Scotia. In 1784, New Brunswick was established as a separate colony to accommodate the English refugees, and it soon became a center for the export of timber and fish to Great Britain. Many of the other Loyalists relocated in and around Montreal or along Lake Ontario. Over the next two decades, a further migration of English Americans to Canada occurred. The motive behind relocation for most of the tens of thousands of these so-called late Loyalists was more economic than political: Free land awaited if they renewed their allegiance to the British monarch.

English immigration to the New World slowed between 1795 and 1815, the period of the Napoleonic Wars, but in the 40 years after Napoléon's defeat, almost 1.5 million British subjects landed at the Canadian ports of Halifax, Nova Scotia; St. John's, Newfoundland; or Quebec City. Although most of them continued on to the United States, hundreds of thousands remained in Canada, where they worked at making habitable what was often an inhospitable land.

The Settlers of Prince Edward Island

One place where they went to work was Prince Edward Island, the smallest province. Originally called the Island of St. John, this region of 2,184 square miles in the

Gulf of St. Lawrence was renamed in 1799 for Queen Victoria's father. Because the island's potential as a shipping center was limited by its smallness and by the proximity of other harbors, at the close of the 18th century it was inhabited by only about 5,000 people, most of them English.

Here, as elsewhere in Canada, the Napoleonic Wars brought change. England was accustomed to obtaining the timber it needed for shipbuilding from Europe, particularly the Baltic nations, but Napoléon's imposition of the Continental System, a continent-wide boycott on trade with Britain, forced the English to seek other alternatives. Consequently, the timber trade in the Maritime Provinces (New Brunswick, Nova Scotia, and Prince Edward Island) and Newfoundland boomed. By 1826, Prince Edward Island had become a shipbuilding center, and its population had grown nearly fivefold, to 23,000 people, a figure that then doubled in the next 20 years. Much of this increase could be attributed to immigration from England.

For the most part, the English settlers of Prince Edward Island came from the northern towns of Devon and Cornwall, among them Appledore, Kilkhampton, and Bideford. About 10,000 of these west countrymen, as they are called, arrived in the 5 decades after 1818; in the 1830s alone, half of the population of the town of Bideford emigrated to Prince Edward Island. The Cornish and Devonish were well familiar with the North Atlantic, having traveled it for centuries as fishermen.

On Prince Edward Island, they learned new work. Some became loggers. Trees were felled from January to March, so as to be ready to be floated downstream during the spring runoff of melted snow and ice. In the off-season, loggers tended small farms for their families. Most loggers lived in wood huts along the creeks that were used to transport lumber. Other English immigrants found work in the island's shipyards, and some worked as commercial fishermen.

Close ties with England enabled Prince Edward Island to prosper. Canadian-made ships, filled with lumber, called regularly at the Bideford docks. Charlottetown, Prince Edward Island's capital and largest town, became the nexus of the new prosperity. Loggers and shipwrights from around the island crowded into its luxury stores to choose from a vast array of English-made goods, including prints, shawls, bonnets, ribbons, parasols, desks, toys, and saddles.

But Prince Edward Island's reliance on timber meant that its prosperity would be short-lived. An iron steamship launched, ironically, from Bideford in 1834, announced the onset of an era in which wooden sailing ships would be obsolete. However, once the forests that covered the island were depleted, the people of Prince Edward Island discovered that the soil underneath was good for farming. Today they raise potatoes, barley, and oats; the island's fishermen still catch fish, lobsters, and oysters. Tourism also helps support the island's 125,000 residents, about one-third of whom still claim English descent.

Prelude of Things to Come

As Canada became more heavily populated and prosperous, its people began to yearn for complete control over their own political affairs. Canadians elected their own local assemblies, but the English government retained the right to appoint a colonial governor. A report on Canada's future filed in 1839 by the earl of Durham, governor general for Canada, proposed that a united Canada be given power over its own affairs. Durham's report formed the basis for England's eventual grant of autonomy to Canada; it has been called "the most valuable document in the English language on the subject of colonial policy." For the first time in world history, independence from an imperial ruler was gained without bloodshed.

Lord Durham, governor general of Canada, proposed in 1839 that a reunified Upper and Lower Canada be granted substantial autonomy to govern its own affairs.

When Canada achieved its autonomy in 1867, its 4 provinces—which constitute just 10 percent of the nation's area today—were home to the same number of citizens as had lived in the 13 colonies when they achieved their independence. In other ways, Canada was more advanced than the United States had been at birth. More than 2,000 miles of track gave it one of the largest railroad networks in the world, its populace was almost universally literate, and its natural resources were the envy of the world.

On the downside, Ontario's farmland was nearing exhaustion, the winters were extremely cold and long, and people living in the sparsely settled countryside often found it to be lonely and isolated. Many moved to the cities in search of industrial work, but an economic slump in the 1870s limited opportunity. Because almost all of the population lived within 100 miles of the U.S. border (this is still true today), it was easy for anyone who wanted to leave to do so. By 1900 one-quarter of the people had done just that. The factory hand's motto, "A dollar a day is very good pay," was true only if he did not consider the two dollars he could earn in Detroit, Chicago, or Buffalo.

But as was also true of the United States, the presence of vast tracts of land in the West enabled Canada to expand. By 1905 the western regions of Manitoba, British Columbia, Saskatchewan, and Alberta were all part of the dominion. These western lands would help Canada absorb the vast numbers of immigrants who came in the early 20th century, and the West's mineral wealth and fertile prairies would become a cornerstone of the Canadian economy.

The Pacific Coast

Sir Francis Drake, in the 1570s, was the first Englishman to skirt Canada's Pacific coast. English settlers did not arrive in the region until 200 years later, when Captain James Cook reached Nootka Sound on Vancouver Island. For 60 years, the fur trade was the West's biggest lure, but mining and forestry were also important to the region. Gold strikes on the Fraser River in 1858 and in the Klondike region of the Yukon Territory in the 1890s brought thousands of eager immigrants west. Many others were drawn by the availability of land suitable for farming; their way was made easier by the completion in 1885 of the Canadian Pacific Railway, which spanned the continent. Until 1900 about two-thirds of the newcomers to the Canadian West hailed from the British Isles, a preponderance of them from England.

Ethnic Tensions

Canadian history has been shaped by the rivalry between its two most populous ethnic groups. Men of

An inn in the Klondike goldfields. The gold rush in the Klondike in the 1890s was profitable not only for the miners lucky enough to strike gold but for the businesses that satisfied their needs.

British origins held the prime ministership from 1867 until 1896, when a French Canadian, Sir Wilfrid Laurier, gained the post. His proposal to open Canada's markets to free trade aroused apprehension among Canadians of English descent that economic ties with Britain would thereby be weakened or that, worse, political union with the United States might result. (Canadians had long feared that the United States had territorial designs on

Canada, and with good reason: In the 19th century, several invasions of Canada were launched from U.S. soil, and American expansionists often discussed adding Canadian territory to the United States. Canadians also feared the economic might of their neighbor to the south.) Resistance to Laurier's proposal was widespread; the opposition leader replied, "A British subject was I born; a British subject I will die." Ontario, the largest and wealthiest province, home by a wide margin to the most English natives, has usually been the locus of this kind of sentiment. The *British Canadian*, a newspaper published in the city of Simcoe from 1860 to 1927, gave voice to these people.

The period of heaviest immigration to Canada, the years between 1890 and 1914, brought several million newcomers. About 1 million of these were English. For a few years in the early 20th century more English immigrants chose Canada than the United States, although a significant number of these eventually migrated south. The main reason for this phenomenon was that although most of the cheap farmland in the United States had already been taken, there was still a lot of acreage available in Canada's Prairie Provinces of Manitoba, Saskatchewan, and Alberta. As a result of the rise in immigration, wheat production there increased sevenfold in just 15 years. At the same time, Ontario's industrial base—and with it shipping on the Great Lakes—was expanding. Although most English workers brought with them ideas about the importance of labor unions and for that reason were sometimes not especially popular with employers, economic opportunity was available in Canada as never before.

The influx of European immigrants made Canadian society much more ethnically diverse. In addition to the English and French and their descendants, Canada was now home to significant communities of Ukrainians, Scandinavians, Germans, Italians, Poles, Dutch, Greeks, Jews, and Russians. Most of these newcomers learned to speak English, making the language their most vital tie to Canadian culture. This was resented by French Canadians, who still clung to the use of French. At times the rivalry between Anglophones (English speakers) and Francophones (French speakers) grew so fierce, particularly in the predominantly French province of Quebec, that it erupted into rioting. A frequent cause of the violence was the reluctance of French Canadians to enlist in the military during times of crisis for the British Empire, such as the Boer War of 1899–1902. In recent decades, many French Canadians have been active in the Quebec separatist movement, which seeks independence for that province.

Thinking Continentally

After 1920, Canada's ties with England grew less strong as it developed its relationship, particularly economically, with the United States. During the Second World War, Canada and the United States signed a joint defense agreement. Despite this shift in focus, English immigrants continued to arrive in Canada—350,000 in the 1920s, 600,000 between 1945 and 1967, and 300,000 since 1970. This last group is significant because for the first time in the history of the English migration to Canada, the number of female immigrants has been almost equal to the number of males. In other ways the recent immigrants are more conventional—as in previous centuries, they tend to be young, between 20 and 35 years of age. Most head for the bigger cities, mainly Toronto, Ottawa, and Vancouver, and steer clear of French-dominated Montreal and Quebec.

In 1989 one-quarter of Canada's 26 million people designated their ancestry as English. An equal proportion regarded themselves as French Canadians. The provinces with the highest percentage of English Canadians are Newfoundland, British Columbia, and Nova Scotia—by no coincidence the first three landing sites of English navigators. More than 2 million people have both English and French forebears. In the 1980s, many Anglophone Canadians began to supplement their mother tongue with French, the other official national language. One in six Anglophones can now speak both.

Like the English in the United States, the English in Canada can be found in every part of their nation, at every level of society, practicing every profession, working at every conceivable kind of job. Like the English in the United States, they can take great pride in the leading role played by themselves, their compatriots, and their ancestors in both the earliest and the most important chapters in their adopted nation's history. Indeed, like the English in the United States, their story is indistinguishable from that of their nation.

A group of happy English war brides and their children wave good-bye to England as the liner Argentina *departs for the United States in 1946.*

A SINGULAR LEGACY

In 1890 there were about 900,000 English-born people in the United States. By 1970 there were just half that many. Immigration to the United States in the 1920s and 1930s dropped to its lowest point in 100 years. Nearly a million British soldiers had been killed in World War I—young men had traditionally been the most likely to emigrate — and in the post–World War I years the English did not even fulfill the immigration quotas drawn by U.S. legislators that favored them above other immigrant groups. Those who did leave England opted for the former or current colonies in Africa, Asia, Australia, or Canada.

Because of their ease in assimilation and the social mobility they enjoyed in comparison with other immigrant groups, immigrants from England have not demonstrated as much ethnic cohesiveness as other groups. In comparison with other ethnic groups in the United States, the English were rarely made to feel unwelcome or unwanted; consequently, they have rarely felt the need to band together. Specifically English-American cultural, social, and political organizations were nonexistent or short-lived. The English rarely found the doors of equivalent American institutions closed to them, and most were able to move easily into the mainstream of American life. Partly as a result, the English Americans showed a greater ability than any other immigrant group to improve themselves economically over generations. A large percentage of the sons and daughters of manual laborers and farmers moved into professional careers. In their personal lives, English Americans showed the same ability to "Americanize." Less than half of the English living in New York in the early 20th century, for example, married another person of English descent.

The War Brides

The outbreak of World War II in 1939 gladdened no one, but it did provide a set of singular circumstances that led to romance and marriage and a new chapter in the history of English immigration to North America. Several thousand Englishwomen married Canadian soldiers who were stationed in Britain during the war; likewise, a small number of English servicemen stationed at U.S. bases or overseas tied the knot with American women. But the most common pairing took place between U.S. soldiers and Englishwomen.

Two million American soldiers were stationed in Great Britain during or after the war, and it is little surprise that in those grim days about 100,000 British women said yes to a marriage proposal from an American GI and eventually came to the United States. About half of these women had served in the British armed forces. Military and government officials tried—with remarkably little success—to discourage such liaisons on the grounds that romance would interfere with the war effort.

Two decades or so earlier, in the few months that American soldiers were stationed in Britain during the First World War, the two peoples did not mix well; British women preferred Canadians or the French, if anyone. In the meantime, cultural differences had narrowed or were more readily overlooked. "We were beginning to realize that under the brashness and puppy-like friendliness of the Americans," said one woman, "were very homesick young men." The sheer size of the American military presence in England made it inevitable that American men and Englishwomen

American GIs dance with English women at a club run by the Red Cross in London during World War II. Many war brides met their future husbands in such clubs.

would meet—at the movies, in pubs, at church, on city buses and trains.

The most frequent meeting place was the Red Cross club. By D day (June 6, 1944), the date of the great Allied invasion of Europe, the American Red Cross had set up more than 250 clubs for servicemen and -women. Saturday night was dance night, and at the largest club, Rainbow Corner in London, the floor accommodated 300 dancers. It was not uncommon for air-raid sirens, announcing another German bombing raid, to interrupt the music, in which case the suitor might then take his date to a nearby air-raid shelter.

England, once a "green and pleasant land," in the words of the poet William Blake, was gray and anxious during the war. The Americans brightened the atmosphere, it seemed. They were, said a war bride from the naval base city of Southampton, "all good looking, had a fantastic sense of humor, seemed to have unlimited spending money. . . . Most were gentlemen at least until the second date, and they all had perfect teeth."

For Englishwomen who married American men during the war, reaching their new home could be as difficult an obstacle as any faced by the first immigrants more than 300 years earlier. German submarines prowled the North Atlantic, and civilian travel was severely restricted. Even so, sympathetic sailors brought 30,000 British brides to U.S. ports during the war, aboard boats carrying injured Americans and German prisoners.

At war's end, paperwork became the obstacle. Every foreigner wishing to immigrate, even if married to a U.S. citizen, was required to wait a certain period, but in December 1945 Congress passed a law designed to expedite the war brides' entry. Much publicity surrounded their arrival, which was hailed as symbolic of the new closeness that had developed between Britain and the United States as the result of their wartime alliance. Six months later, another law hastened the entry of many thousands of British fiancées.

An English-born woman who has lived in New Jersey since that period, Madeline Sands, said recently, "It's funny that they called us 'war brides.' I didn't marry the war, I married my husband, and we and the children are glad of it. We've visited my family a few times, but all in all I think of myself as an American."

English or American?

Like many immigrants of every nationality, thousands of English in America never changed their citizenship, opting to return home or to live on in America as British subjects. One contributor to *The Forum* of New York, in March 1900, who signed himself F. Cunliffe-Owen, offered an explanation that is revelatory of one aspect of the English-American experience. He asserted that of all the foreign-born persons living in the United States, "the Englishman, especially the Englishman of the better class . . . as a general rule refrains from taking any steps to become a citizen." The reason? "There is so much sympathy between our two countries . . . the system of law and justice being almost identical, that it is possible for us Englishmen in America to remain loyal to our Queen." A different viewpoint was provided by a more recent arrival from England, Dudley Stone. "I came to the United States in 1969," said this immigrant. "My wife was born in France, but our daughter is American, and I realized I was never leaving, so I became a citizen." From this man's perspective as a part-time actor, Americans have only a superficial understanding of the English. "The directors want me to be a Hollywood Englishman, to act a certain way and play up the accent," he says. "*No one* in England talks that way. Can't they just see me as another person?"

Even before World War II, laborers and farmers had come to constitute only a very small percentage of all English immigrants, a trend that was accelerated when U.S. immigration laws changed in the 1950s to favor people with technical or special skills. Most of the

English machinist Alan Stopford left his homeland for better prospects in Baltimore, Maryland. He was one of 50 skilled English machinists recruited by the Koppers Company in the late 1960s.

400,000 English who have been admitted to the United States since 1960 (roughly 10 percent of all immigrants) fall into that category. In the early 1960s more physicians and surgeons came to the United States from England than from any other nation. More recently, several thousand engineers, technicians, and programmers from England have added to the spectacular success of the computer industry in California's Silicon Valley and Boston's Route 128. Nurses, administrators, accountants, secretaries, teachers, have all been part of the "brain drain" of talented English emigrants. These new English immigrants invariably possess a fine education and other advantages, and the social mobility that the English in America have always enjoyed makes it comparatively easy for them to acclimate.

Why do the English continue to leave their homeland? John Edwards, a London resident who works in the financial services industry and is married to an American, put it this way. "England is a crowded little island, and the States has all those open spaces," he said, explaining his plans to emigrate. "I could be earning a good deal more at a comparable job in the States. Plus, I'm not so fond of the Queen and all those royals—'Viva la Republic' is my motto, and the States seems like the least class-conscious place." He and his wife plan to live in Boston, her hometown, or on the West Coast. Those choices are in keeping with current trends: The most popular destinations for English immigrants since 1970 have been Massachusetts, New York, and California, especially their major cities.

A Dual Legacy

Six generations of English immigrants came to North America before the American Revolution. Since 1776 eight more generations have come. Like the pre-Revolution groups, they came for a variety of reasons. There were religiously motivated individuals, such as the Puritans. There were people who came for political reasons, for adventure, and for love and family.

Most of all they came, like every other national or ethnic group that has ventured to America over that same period, for economic reasons. Throughout North America's brief history, its primary allure has been the promise of a job, better wages, open land, or a more immediate return on invested money.

But if in that respect the English-American experience is similar to that of other immigrant groups, in other ways it is absolutely unique. The English and their ideas about government, culture, religion, and commerce shaped the United States and Canada more significantly than any other immigrant group. After all,

At Pickwick's, a restaurant in Woodland Hills, California, the owners have attempted to recreate the atmosphere of a British pub.

the homeland of no other immigrant group once ruled both the United States and Canada as colonies. Although the English were the most numerous immigrant group only between 1500 and 1783, the foundation of their influence had already been established through their role in creating the characteristic institutions of American life. Examples beyond those already discussed are legion. Baseball, America's national pastime, has its roots in the English schoolboy's game of rounders. In music, English folk songs were carried by English Americans from the Atlantic shore to the hills and valleys of Kentucky and Tennessee. Coupled with labor union chants and ballads of the late 19th and early 20th centuries, that tradition survives to the present day through the music of such quintessentially American musicians as Woody Guthrie and Bob Dylan. Until the 1970s, the English country manor served as the principal model for Americans building an estate, and it is still favored by many architects.

The list could go on forever. Strange, then, that so influential a group could be considered the invisible immigrants. Yet it may be not so peculiar when one considers that the most crucial question faced by virtually every other immigrant group is the degree to which it will assimilate—that is, absorb, or be absorbed by, American culture in all its myriad permutations. The same challenge is faced, to a certain extent, by the more recent English immigrants, but earlier arrivals— the English who played the lead role in settling North America—had to resolve no such conflict. Instead, by virtue of an immutable and more mysterious process, they became a new people, one that had never existed before — Americans—and created a new nation. The very notion of "Americanness" by which assimilation is measured can therefore be seen as part of the English influence, which is elsewhere written on every page of American history. Other peoples have come to America; the enduring English legacy is that, more than any other people, they invented it.

FURTHER READING

Bailyn, Bernard. *The Peopling of British North America: An Introduction.* New York: Knopf, 1986.

———. *The New England Merchants in the Seventeenth Century.* New York: Harper & Row, 1964.

Berthoff, Rowland T. *British Immigrants in Industrial America, 1790–1950.* Cambridge: Harvard University Press, 1953.

Blumenthal, Shirley, and Jerome S. Ozer. *Coming to America: Immigrants from the British Isles.* New York: Delacorte, 1980.

Erickson, Charlotte. *Invisible Immigrants: The Adaptation of British and Scottish Immigrants in 19th-Century America.* Miami: University of Miami Press, 1972.

Fischer, David H. *Albion's Seed.* New York: Oxford University Press, 1989.

Shukert, Elfrieda, and Barbara Scibetta. *The War Brides of World War II.* New York: Penguin Books, 1989.

Trevelyan, G. M. *A Shortened History of England.* New York: Penguin Books, 1986.

Wertenbaker, Thomas Jefferson. *The First Americans, 1607–1690.* New York: Macmillan, 1927.

INDEX

PICTURE CREDITS

JAMES M. CORNELIUS is a writer and editor in New York City. His book reviews have appeared in *Publishers Weekly*, the *New York Times Book Review*, the *Cleveland Plain Dealer*, and the *Minneapolis Tribune*.

DANIEL PATRICK MOYNIHAN is the senior United States senator from New York. He is also the only person in American history to serve in the cabinets or subcabinets of four successive presidents—Kennedy, Johnson, Nixon, and Ford. Formerly a professor of government at Harvard University, he has written and edited many books, including *Beyond the Melting Pot*, *Ethnicity: Theory and Experience* (both with Nathan Glazer), *Loyalties*, and *Family and Nation*.